Lyotard and Politics

THINKING POLITICS

Series Editors: Geoff M. Boucher and Matthew Sharpe

Politics in the twenty-first century is immensely complex and multi-faceted, and alternative theorisations of debates that radically renew older ideas have grown from a trickle to a flood in the past twenty years. The most interesting and relevant contemporary thinkers have responded to new political challenges – such as liberal multiculturalism, new directions in feminist thinking, theories of global empire and biopolitical power, and challenges to secularism – by widening the scope of their intellectual engagements and responding to the new politics. The thinkers selected for inclusion in the series have all responded to the urgency and complexity of thinking about politics today in fresh ways.

Books in the series will provide clear and accessible introductions to the major ideas in contemporary thinking about politics, through a focus in each volume on a key political thinker. Rather than a roll-call of the 'usual suspects' it will focus on new thinkers who offer provocative new directions and some neglected older thinkers whose relevance is becoming clear as a result of the changing situation.

Each book will:

- Provide a summary overview of the thinker's contribution
- Position the thinker within the contemporary political field and their intellectual contexts
- Explain key concepts and events
- Balance accessibility with a serious critical treatment of the thinker
- Expose the thinker's ideas to robust tests of empirical and conceptual evidence
- Focus on ideas and debates in relation to real world politics and contemporary political questions with empirical examples
- Include text boxes to highlight key concepts and figures

Published titles
Agamben and Politics: A Critical Introduction
Sergei Prozorov

Foucault and Politics: A Critical Introduction
Mark G. E. Kelly

Taylor and Politics: A Critical Introduction
Craig Browne and Andrew P. Lynch

Habermas and Politics: A Critical Introduction
Matheson Russell

Irigaray and Politics: A Critical Introduction
Laura Roberts

https://edinburghuniversitypress.com/series-thinking-politics.html

LYOTARD AND POLITICS
A CRITICAL INTRODUCTION

Stuart Sim

EDINBURGH
University Press

Edinburgh University Press is one of the leading university presses in the UK. We publish academic books and journals in our selected subject areas across the humanities and social sciences, combining cutting-edge scholarship with high editorial and production values to produce academic works of lasting importance. For more information visit our website: edinburghuniversitypress.com

Edinburgh University Press Ltd
The Tun – Holyrood Road
12(2f) Jackson's Entry
Edinburgh EH8 8PJ

Typeset in 11/13 Adobe Sabon by
IDSUK (DataConnection) Ltd

A CIP record for this book is available from the British Library

ISBN 978 1 4744 5651 7 (hardback)
ISBN 978 1 4744 5653 1 (webready PDF)
ISBN 978 1 4744 5652 4 (paperback)
ISBN 978 1 4744 5654 8 (epub)

Contents

Acknowledgements

My thanks go to Jen Daly and Sarah Foyle at Edinburgh University Press for handling the project so efficiently through its various stages; it is always a pleasure to work with EUP, with which I have had a long and fruitful relationship going back over twenty years now. The series editors, Geoff Boucher and Matthew Sharpe, provided helpful comments on the proposal, and the peer review process gave constructive advice regarding revisions. As ever, Dr Helene Brandon was supportive throughout the whole writing process and an attentive sounding board for the book's arguments.

Introduction

Thinking Politics with Lyotard

It is the political dimension to Jean-François Lyotard's work that more than anything else makes him stand out from his poststructuralist and postmodernist contemporaries. He is invariably 'thinking politics', concerned to find ways of translating philosophical thought into a basis for political action, as in his concepts of the 'little narrative', 'paganism' and the 'differend'. Lyotard is most famous for his attack on 'grand narratives' in *The Postmodern Condition*, denouncing these as outdated and not worthy of any further support; but his work as a whole represents a consistent critique of the power structures of contemporary culture, revealing him to be a thinker resolutely opposed to systems claiming universal application and brooking no opposition to those claims. It is a point he is quite adamant about, declaring that 'it is high time that philosophers abandon the hope of producing a unitary theory as the last word on things. There is no *archè*, nor does the Good exist as a unitary horizon'.[1] This cast to his thought is evident from his earliest writings on the Algerian Revolution in the 1950s, where he was critical of both the French state for its colonialist policies and the communist oriented rebel forces (Front de libération nationale, FLN) fighting against it to achieve Algerian independence, through to his reflections on the threat posed by techno-science in *The Inhuman*, with its nightmare scenario of a universe in which computers were to outlive humanity, having been designed to do so by the techno-capitalistic corporate sector. When it comes to authority, Lyotard's default position is firmly anti- and he develops a distinctive brand of pragmatism with which to oppose the institutional and ideological forces wielding this power. He is always thinking tactically in relation to grand narratives, seeking out ways to undermine their influence and show up their failings and false claims, his point being that no grand narrative can deliver what it promises because it is based on a false assumption as to the extent of its power, particularly its ability to control events. That is every grand narrative's weak point, and Lyotard is tireless in drawing our attention to it; for him it is a reason to dispense with the

1

notion altogether and construct a new method of conducting politics that is free of the shackles of both authority and tradition.

This project's brief is to explore how a Lyotardean pragmatism, based on relativist principles, can provide a focus for political theory and action in a cultural climate featuring a dramatic resurgence of right-wing extremism (a phenomenon that Lyotard would have been concerned, but not at all surprised, by). As he notes in *The Postmodern Condition* of how pragmatism informs his analytical technique, 'What is required of a working hypothesis is a fine capacity for discrimination', rather than a foundational ground of the kind that grand narratives simply assume – and that Western philosophy regards as essential to the act of theorising.[2] Working hypotheses will constitute Lyotard's *modus operandi*; the more his career as a thinker develops, then the less he wants to be tied to any set ideological position that would restrict his options. To put it in traditional, colloquial terms, Lyotard is not a 'clubbable' type of person. Even in his early days as a political activist when influenced by Marxism, he comes across as more than something of an outsider, one never quite aligned to the theory's requirements. Although he is subsequently to be identified with the postmodern movement (if not altogether fairly, as we shall go on to see) Lyotard has an abiding distrust of 'isms': working hypotheses will always lead him away from these. He wants to address all political issues without preconceptions, the very opposite of what followers of a grand narrative like Marxism would do.

Lyotard's rejection of universal theories and of the need for there to be a ground to his philosophical thinking marks him out as a sceptically oriented thinker, but inevitably raises the issue of how to justify making value judgements at all if you are a relativist. It is a difficulty all sceptics have found themselves confronted by from classical times onwards. Being a committed relativist makes him particularly suspicious of the value judgements that those in authority claim to have the right to make, as well as to impose on others, although he is very aware that rejection alone is not a very sustainable position for the critic. There have to be some positive suggestions made in such instances as to how to resist the grand narrative in question and some sort of basis for the value judgement that would, at the very least implicitly, entail. Lyotard's concern to come up with these constitutes one of the most compelling aspects of his philosophical thought. It is a problem that he is always striving to devise ways round, of being able to justify judgements, even without a ground to fall back on, so that others will be persuaded by his line of argument. He does so with considerable conviction in *Heidegger and "the jews"*, for example, his memorable contribution to the 'Heidegger Affair' that created such heated debate in the French intellectual establishment in the 1980s, as to whether that philosopher's well-documented connections with the Nazi regime in Germany (including membership of the Nazi Party itself) invalidated his work or not. Lyotard insisted that Nazism had to be held to account and judged, even by relativists, and Heidegger had to come into that judgement at some point. Relativism did not, and should not, permit one to opt out of such a situation. I will be considering the validity of his response to this issue and its implications for the resurgence of fascism as a political movement throughout Europe, as well as the various forms of populism that have come in its wake. Like Lyotard, we have to find a way of confronting the fascist mindset, with its populist campaigning tactics, to prevent it from poisoning our political life any further than it currently has contrived to do, whether we are relativists or not: an increasingly necessary task in an era when, as Benjamin Moffitt has pointed out, its sophisticated use of the 'new media technologies' has turned into a prevailing *'political style'* on the international stage.[3] It is a style that runs counter to everything that Lyotard believed in politically, appealing directly to people's prejudices and striving as hard as it can to reinforce these. Sceptics and relativists have to enter the fray when that happens.

Lyotard's concept of the differend also addresses the issue of value judgement, in this case when disputes arise that admit of no clear-cut solution because of the incompatible worldviews of the parties involved.[4] He firmly opposes the tendency, so often seen in practice, for the stronger of the two parties to enforce a solution based on its ideological supremacy, using its own rules to the detriment of its opponent. This is a situation that repeatedly arises in world politics – every colonial episode features it to at least some degree, for example – and Lyotard's work therefore continues to resonate, as does his concept of 'the pagan' with its arguments for fluidity of belief and the need for localised belief systems that do not encroach on those of their neighbours.[5] The relation of such thought to the confused geopolitical situation of the present day merits being looked at more closely, fitting into the global versus local debate that has taken on new layers of complexity of late with the rise of nationalism as a counter to globalisation – as seen to particular effect in the 'America First' notion promoted so bombastically, and unfortunately so successfully in electoral terms, by President Donald Trump. Nationalism may appear to be an assertion of the local, but it is generally based on grand narrative principles that claim special privileges for its followers, as America First unashamedly does. That is not what Lyotard had in mind for the pagan, which requires at the very least mutual respect for other social and political systems – provided they do not encroach on one's own. Lyotard is a thinker who invariably shies away from mass movements and universalising theories, being too independently minded to share their assumptions.

Lyotard's place in the development of post-Marxism also invites assessment, considering how his thought (as outlined in works such as *Libidinal Economy*) compares to such other influential theorists in this area as Ernesto Laclau and Chantal Mouffe, with their call for a 'radical democratic politics' to replace Marxist theoretical orthodoxy.[6] Whether the post-Marxist turn in later twentieth-century cultural theory has been a help or a hindrance to left politics is a topic that very much needs to be considered. This is especially the case given the recent return of overtly fascist political groupings throughout Western society and the significant electoral inroads they have been making that the left has seemed unable to curb (very much an ongoing issue throughout Europe as I write, in various individual countries as well as the EU parliament). The question arises as to whether post-Marxism is merely a symptom of Marxism's decline in the face of widespread cultural change ('that vaguely outmoded discourse', as Lyotard was dismissively to refer to it a few years before Laclau and Mouffe's critique),[7] or whether it offers a new mode of thinking and campaigning tactics for the left: a new working hypothesis perhaps? Lyotard's work can be very instructive on this score, revealing the often highly disorienting changes of direction that left-wing thinkers have found themselves being forced to contemplate in the wake of Marxism's decline. The nagging problem of how to construct a left-wing politics in the absence of a left grand narrative of the kind that Marxism had provided for most of the twentieth century, lies at the centre of Lyotard's philosophical output.

The overall aim of this book is to draw out the political implications of Lyotard's major concepts to determine the extent of their applicability to the chaotic world of twenty-first-century politics. To that end I will engage in some thought experiments along the way as to what politics might look like were Lyotard's ideas to be put into operation. What would a parliamentary system based on the little narrative principle look like, for example? Or a justice system that operated, as Lyotard believes a pagan one should, with 'no criteria but opinions' in the creation of its decisions?[8] There will be both advantages and disadvantages to report, but these are certainly worth weighing up against what the current system's institutions are providing. My argument will be that Lyotard offers a way of rethinking some of the most critical ideological conflicts that we are now experiencing (populism, as a notable case in point, plus the dangers posed by the explosive growth of the AI and robotics sector), and that at the very least he is raising the right kind of questions about these – questions more of us should be asking and debating on a regular basis. The political dimension to all his work, including his extensive writings on art (translated into English in several volumes over the last few years) will be emphasised throughout, to demonstrate the extent to which 'thinking politics' is for Lyotard the primary rationale of being a philosopher. The trajectory of the book is therefore designed to take us over the politics of, respectively, relativism, post-Marxism, the differend, the 'Heidegger Affair', the future, aesthetics and the event: topics which mark out the critical core of Lyotard's thought.

Lyotard's Style

Before launching into an analysis of Lyotard's philosophical concerns and beliefs, a brief digression into the issue of style in his work would seem to be in order, because one of the reasons it is so difficult to pin down Lyotard as a theorist is a writing style which differs markedly from what we are used to in philosophical discourse in the English-speaking world. At any one point or other Lyotard's style can be poetic (sometimes in a distinctly flowery way quite at odds with the seriousness of his topic), ironic, laced with invective, or highly personal. He can also get carried away by his rhetoric on occasion, as even he was to admit was the case in *Libidinal Economy*, prompting one commentator (and a supportive one at that) to dub it 'a somewhat violent and scandalous book'.[9] To start a work of philosophy with a description of the dissection of the human body, as he does in that latter text, is, to say the least, novel. Academic philosophical writing in the English-speaking world, on the other hand, tends towards the dry, the abstract and the impersonal, generally putting forward a theory or interpretation and then following it through step by step to a logical conclusion. Lyotard, however, rarely operates in such a straightforward manner; his arguments can wander and his theories and concepts are not always as precise as they could be, or as we would expect to find in English-language philosophy. Margaret

Grebowicz's observation that, when it comes to his writings on the subject of gender, Lyotard is guilty of 'giving the reader no explicit definitions or analyses', such that she is 'left scrambling to pose the "right" questions, to make the appropriate linkages', could stand for his work in general (and once again it is worth noting that this is a sympathetic commentator speaking).[10] Lyotard's thought drifts and that is entirely intentional on his part; as he puts it in the introduction to the collection of his essays in *Driftworks*: 'Driftworks in the plural, for the question is not of leaving *one* shore, but several, simultaneously; what is at work is not one current, pushing and tugging, but different drives and tractions', and those drives and tractions will be a constant presence throughout his writings.[11]

Lyotard has forebears as far as style goes in the continental tradition, such as Friedrich Nietzsche, and contemporaries there too, as in Jacques Derrida, whose writing style and philosophical method have come in for a great deal of criticism amongst the English-speaking philosophical community, striking many as tortuous and lacking in what they take to be the requisite philosophical rigour. Continental philosophy, as it has come to be known, is simply not professional to those trained in the Anglo-American analytical school. Lyotard may not be as opaque as Derrida seems so intent on being so much of the time, but he does make his reader work to determine the rationale behind his often oblique approach to political issues, as well as the overall pattern to his thought. Lyotard has no interest in presenting a unified body of work to the reader, however, but with having an impact on the reader's thought and actions: 'What is important in a text is not what it means, but what it does and incites to do'.[12] What he wants it to do is to incite us to think politics as he does: that is, without preconceptions.

Such qualifications notwithstanding, a case can be made for the value of Lyotard's writing style in terms of relating his work to the contemporary political scene. Kiff Bamford has referred to 'the multiplicity of voices he adopted in order to avoid any sense of a static, complete "theory"' and this is a trait that runs through Lyotard's work, where working hypotheses take the place of theoretical specifics.[13] The great virtue of working hypotheses is that they can be changed, or shed, as circumstances develop: from Lyotard's point of view they more or less have to be. The critical point is to keep moving on to ensure one does not become trapped in a grand narrative that predetermines one's response. Lyotard is the most flexible of political thinkers and in a period when political positions have become ever more extreme and resistant to change, and grand narratives correspondingly more dogmatic in manner, there is much to recommend about an approach based on working hypotheses and a deliberate lack of specifics. Lyotard's many voices challenge us to explore political issues from as many angles as we can and to keep our options open; never to allow ourselves to become boxed in by the demands of a grand narrative. We must always remember that this is an author for whom 'everything in linguistic material leads honest intention to signify astray and betrays loyalty to meaning. The voice can never be done with trying to master rebellious language'.[14] Or rebellious politics either, one could say.

Notes

1. Lyotard, *Discourse, Figure*, p. 14.
2. Lyotard, *The Postmodern Condition*, p. 7.
3. Moffitt, *The Global Rise of Populism*, p. 3.
4. See Lyotard, *The Differend*.
5. See Lyotard, 'Lessons in Paganism', in *The Lyotard Reader*, pp. 122–54.
6. See Laclau and Mouffe, *Hegemony and Socialist Strategy*.
7. Lyotard, *Peregrinations*, p. 54.
8. Lyotard and Thébaud, *Just Gaming*, p. 27.
9. Bennington, *Lyotard: Writing the Event*, p. 1.
10. Grebowicz, 'Introduction: After Lyotard', in Grebowicz, *Gender After Lyotard*, pp. 1–11 (p. 2).
11. Lyotard, *Driftworks*, p. 10.
12. Ibid., p. 9.
13. Bamford, *Lyotard and the 'Figural' in Performance, Art and Writing*, p. 8.
14. Lyotard, *Soundproof Room*, p. 32.

Chapter 1

'Philosophical Politics' in the Twenty-first Century

One of Lyotard's books is entitled *Why Philosophize?* and the short
answer as far as his own career is concerned is: politics. He is always
at pains to emphasise the political dimension of his work, defining
himself as a practitioner of what he calls a 'philosophical politics',
where his stated objective is

> [t]o defend and illustrate philosophy in its differend with its two
> adversaries: on its outside, the genre of economic discourse (exchange,
> capital); on its inside, the genre of academic discourse (mastery). By
> showing that the linking of one phrase onto another is problematic and
> that this problem is the problem of politics, to set up a philosophical
> politics apart from the politics of 'intellectuals' and of politicians. To
> bear witness to the differend.[1]

The implications of this concept in a political climate in which
the far right is asserting itself so aggressively will be discussed in
this chapter, as will its potential to reinvigorate left-wing political
theory and practice to counter this very disturbing phenomenon.
(Bertolt Brecht's warning, with reference to the defeat of Hitler and
the Nazis, 'But don't rejoice too soon at your escape – / The womb
he crawled from still is going strong', seems only too apposite to
our current situation, unfortunately enough.)[2] The extent to which
postmodernism still has a contribution to make to the development
of our culture needs to be brought into the survey as well, especially given Lyotard's reputation as the most overtly political of the
poststructuralist-postmodernist generation of thinkers. He can even
go so far as to assert that 'I do not believe myself to be a philosopher, in the proper sense of the term, but a "politician"', also noting
that 'the meaning of the word "politician" must be completely overhauled'.[3] As a 'politician', Lyotard sees himself as operating outside
the traditional party system, which to his mind means individual
subservience to the party line and the grand narrative it upholds –
Marxism being a prime example of this in action, although all major

political parties demand that kind of loyalty to at least some extent, even if they may not be quite as vindictive against supposed apostates. It is that political edge that I am arguing keeps Lyotard's work resonating so profoundly into our own century.

Lyotard's insistence that our thinking should always remain flexible and open to change is a line that he pursues consistently throughout his work, as in, for example, *The Postmodern Condition* (where the model is 'postmodern' scientific practice), *Just Gaming* (with his concept of the pagan) and *Peregrinations* (the concept of clouds). It is particularly pertinent to recent political debate, where ideological positions have been hardening and becoming increasingly resistant to any notion of compromise – or even negotiation between opposing sides, from where some accommodation between differing worldviews might be found. Lyotard's political thinking runs directly counter to that trend, being intrinsically geared towards the defence of difference, and can be built on by the left as a way of responding to it in a creative fashion. 'Politics is not everything', he insists, 'if by that one believes it to be the genre that contains all genres. It is not *a* genre'.[4] Capitalism in its most recent incarnation, neoliberalism, really does believe that all social and political genres collapse into it and that it holds the key to humanity's development, and philosophical politics will adopt an adversarial position towards all such claims to constitute an ultimate expression. Philosophical politics plays out as a series of tactical moves rather than an ideological position in its own right, although as with any sceptically biased theory it is always clear what it is against. Lyotard is to make a significant contribution to the history of sceptical thought through his adroit use of those tactical skills, and it will be one of the main aims of this book to bring that out.

Philosophers and Intellectuals

If we should be aware of subtle differences between being a philosopher and a politician, we should be even more aware of those same differences between philosophers and intellectuals. Intellectuals, in Lyotard's way of thinking, are those who take sides in the political arena and provide arguments for suppressing difference – as much of a problem on the left as the right, it has to be said:

> If philosophers agree to help their fellow citizens in authority in matters where there isn't any, to legitimate this authority, then they cease to ponder in the sense of which I spoke of thinking, and they thereby

9

cease to be philosophers. They become what one calls intellectuals, that is, persons who legitimate a claimed competence . . . And then they all fill the same role, even if some are Catholic and others free thinkers or Marxists, even if some are on the left and others on the right.[5]

Philosophical politics eschews such extreme partisanship, rejecting the notion that there is only one right way of reaching a settlement to any political disagreement, since that involves a denial of the claims of difference through a refusal to bear witness to the differend: 'One side's legitimacy does not imply the other's lack of legitimacy', as Lyotard puts it, pinpointing one of the most persistent flaws of grand narrative politics.[6] Yet throughout history intellectuals have all too often been prepared to come up with arguments that it does and to support regimes that suppress opposition to their ideological programme – a characteristic that most regimes are only too likely to develop, even within the liberal democratic sector. To Lyotard, that is a betrayal of the philosophical ethos as he understands it, and he is quite blunt in specifying why he thinks so: 'You can't be a philosopher (not even a teacher of philosophy) if your mind is made up on a question before you arrive'.[7] That is what intellectuals are guilty of in his opinion: taking received beliefs at face value rather than thinking them through, as they ought to feel themselves under an obligation to do. Lyotard can be decidedly moralistic when it comes to legitimating a claimed competence; that should never be the business of philosophy.

By espousing a philosophical politics, Lyotard maintains a tradition of the philosopher as a public figure in French life that can be seen in the generation before him in Jean-Paul Sartre and the existentialist movement (although he can be very critical of Sartre and the style of intellectual that he came to embody). Sartre had a very high public profile and his pronouncements on public affairs carried a considerable amount of authority; but philosophical politics has a very different conception of what it means to be an intellectual and what is required of such a figure in the public arena, one that resists being in any way authoritative. In Lyotard's case, he sees himself as operating in an era where there is a 'weariness with regard to "theory"' that he feels compelled to find a way around.[8] His objective is to reconnect philosophy with the public realm: 'The time has come to philosophize', as he puts it in the Preface to The Differend.[9] What that involves for Lyotard is demonstrating how there can never be a discourse that explains everything, or that allows interested parties to control it in order to further their ideological aims, hence his claim that '[t]here ought no longer to be "intellectuals"' pretending that there is.[10] Something within the discourse will always prevent such a state from arising, and philosophers have a duty to keep reminding the public that this is so – particularly since those interested parties will invariably refuse to admit there is any problem at all in this regard and that they alone possess the magic formula to resolve all socio-political discord, the exclusive rights to legitimacy. It is a point I will be returning to frequently over the course of this study: the key to Lyotard's uncompromising denial of the validity of universal theories, a position which situates him on the outside of both right- and left-wing orthodoxy – as well as most of his philosophical peers (certainly those in the non-continental tradition).

Lyotard's Postmodernism

Lyotard has played an important role in the development of poststructuralist and postmodernist thought, particularly through the impact of *The Postmodern Condition*. This 'Report on Knowledge' turned into one of the most influential and heavily cited works of cultural theory of the later twentieth century, although as various commentators have pointed out since its English translation in 1984, it is not the most characteristic of Lyotard's books ('arguably unrepresentative', as Graham Jones and Ashley Woodward put it)[11] and he is in fact fairly ambivalent towards postmodernism as a theoretical movement. Jones also points out, however, that as 'the notion of the postmodern advanced by Lyotard has little to do with the way most people use or understand this term', we should be alert to the difference and recognise that for him it signifies a recurrent cultural pattern, not some mere passing fad.[12] It is yet another word which needs its meaning 'overhauled'. As he kept insisting through to the end of his career, for Lyotard the modern and the postmodern have a symbiotic relationship to each other:

> [N]either modernity nor so-called postmodernity can be identified and defined as clearly circumscribed historical entities, of which the latter would always come 'after' the former. Rather we have to say that the postmodern is always implied in the modern because of the fact that modernity, modern temporality, comprises in itself an impulsion to exceed itself into a state other than itself.[13]

Even if it just as a commentator, and one with reservations such as the above, Lyotard still played a significant role in how postmodernism developed as a theoretical position, and his conception of the term is actually a much richer one than the more common understanding of it as a reaction to a particular ideology. The larger cultural context in which Lyotard places the postmodern indicates that the debate about its nature cannot be considered over; in a sense the postmodern is always with us and we need to factor that into our political theorising. 'Arguably unrepresentative' or not, Lyotard has to come into any discussion of the postmodern.

Poststructuralist and postmodernist thinkers are often criticised for being negative in their theorising, however, seemingly more concerned with undermining existing political systems and institutions than in constructing viable alternatives to them. After a while it can become to seem something of a game, losing its force as a political statement in consequence – a criticism that can be levelled at Jacques Derrida in particular. Lyotard is a notable exception to this tendency, and he consistently sought to engage himself politically, arguing the merits of practising a philosophical politics, whereby philosophers helped to give voice to those oppressed by the grand narratives of their culture and unable to articulate their grievances well enough to effect a change of their condition. Differends abound and need to be brought out into the open. Crucially, this was to be a process carried out without the philosophers espousing any grand narrative themselves, as intellectual politics was disposed to do. The concept of little narrative was designed specifically to generate resistance to the governing bodies and institutions within society: at the very least to suggest tactics for such an activity, rather than to construct a rival ideology. It called for short-term, targeted campaigns to challenge particular abuses of power and that idea has intriguing implications for the contemporary political situation, where issues such as Brexit and the Trump presidency have proved to be socially extremely divisive, with respect for difference being one of the main casualties of the bitterly fought debates that have ensued. In consequence, little narrative groupings have been springing up in opposition, both on the left and the right (and to some extent also within the main political parties in the West, as with the Momentum movement within the UK's Labour Party, or the European Research Group within its Conservative Party). Lyotard conceived of little narratives as basically left-wing and libertarian in character and would not have approved of far right-wing versions, which actively work to suppress difference, and if possible eradicate it altogether. I will explore the phenomenon in general to establish the ways in which far-right versions fail to meet Lyotard's requirements for little narrative projects and thus have to be opposed by the left to prevent the marginalisation of difference in the political domain. Immigrants are very much in the front line of that unpleasant process and it is the attitude towards difference that will define the nature of each project. Respect for, and defence of, difference are essential elements of political life for Lyotard and he will judge all movements accordingly.

The positive and negative aspects of little narratives need to be weighed up carefully, therefore, as well as considering whether such entities fit into the current wave of populism – particularly the notion of 'left populism' put forward by such critical theorists as Chantal Mouffe as an antidote to the fascist version now so much in evidence on the European political scene.[14] To some extent little narratives might be considered to have a populist character as well, as anyone who agrees with their overall objective can participate in the campaign that ensues, even if they might differ from their fellow members on party political grounds: so-called 'rainbow coalitions' can emerge in such instances (environmental concerns often attract just such groupings that cut across existing party lines). Yet, as we shall see, little narratives have an in-built resistance to developing into mass movements, whereas populism will always aspire to that condition. The latter's goal is to dominate the political realm and gain ruling power, not simply to be a protest movement that is here today and gone tomorrow. Lyotard is always wary of difference being lost in such a shift where the particular finds itself being subsumed under the general; his sympathies invariably will lie with the former, and his version of postmodernism is designed to bring difference and the particular to the fore in whatever political debate may arise. Given that difference is under such attack at present from dogmatically minded forces on the right, that makes Lyotard's thinking on this issue all the more relevant to the contemporary political scene.

Peregrinations: *Thinking Politics Fluidly*

Fluidity and flexibility of thought and belief are what come through particularly strongly in *Peregrinations*, where Lyotard likens the movement of thought to that of clouds, an amorphous entity in a permanent state of change and flux that can never be pinned down or regarded as complete:

> Thoughts are not the fruits of the earth. They are not registered by areas, except out of human commodity. Thoughts are clouds. The periphery of

thoughts is as immeasurable as the fractal lines of Benoit Mandelbrot. Thoughts are pushed and pulled at variable speeds . . . Thoughts never stop changing their location one with the other.[15]

The implications of that view for political life are fairly obvious: there can be no way of marking out a position that will hold indefinitely and it would be counter-productive even to try: 'It is a delusion to give a meaning to an event or imagine a meaning for an event by anticipating what that event will be in reference to a pre-text'.[16] Lyotard sees his own career as having unfolded in just such an unpredictable and rather haphazard manner, with no immediately recognisable overall pattern to it. Instead, events just happened and he responded to them as the situation appeared to require and his circumstances allowed. He became a father and therefore needed a job, which led him to take up a teaching post in Algeria, then a French colony, which led in turn to becoming a commentator on the Algerian Revolution for the Socialisme ou Barbarie collective. That for Lyotard is what politics is actually like, rather than a process that can be manipulated at will by any particular party in order to control their society. There are simply too many variables involved for the latter to work indefinitely; events will just keep getting in the way to disrupt even the most carefully worked out plans. As Lyotard notes, 'Neither the Commune nor May 1968 were heard coming, sounding notes of preparation'.[17] Both the far right and the far left still operate as if it were possible to exert such ideological control, however, and treat it as a matter of overcoming opposition to their planned programme of action in order to clear the way to be able to do so. Much of Western politics is conducted on that premise, as if events like May 1968 could be written off as mere freak accidents. Lyotard, on the other hand, will emphasise the sheer contingency of human existence in general and continue to champion 'interventions of the *here and now* kind' rather than following any revolutionary rule book as to how to proceed.[18] There is no 'end to history' to be expected, whether of the Marxist utopian kind or its bourgeois equivalent, liberal democracy's supposed triumph over all other ideologies as claimed by theorists like Francis Fukuyama:[19] that, to Lyotard, is one of the abiding myths of political theory that has led to so much trouble and suffering over humankind's history. Postmodern thought in general is dedicated to the subversion of such ideas, in whatever area of human endeavour they are to be found at work. The future is always open for such thinkers and politics always in a state of flux; nothing has been predetermined, everything is to play for at every stage of the proceedings. As Lyotard rather dramatically puts it in *The Inhuman*, 'Being prepared to receive what thought is not prepared to think is what deserves the name of thinking', and his receptiveness is to keep him in a confrontational position with establishment thought in general.[20] Neither Brexit nor Trump supporters, as cases in point, have been prepared to do that and politics has been all the worse for it; right populism thrives in such an atmosphere. The presence or otherwise of that receptiveness will be another way Lyotard has of judging political positions; uncritical belief is to be considered the enemy.

Left Populism

Mouffe's left populism is presented as an acceptable form of the populist impulse that can overturn, or at the very least reduce the impact of, the resurgent right-wing variety enough to help reset political life. For Mouffe, it is a process of harnessing all the opposition to the establishment that exists in order to create a united front to seek political reform. The notion is that this would attract wider public support if it opened the political system to a greater range of voices, thus curbing the power of the elite to a significant degree. This effectively amounts to a restatement of the ideals of radical democracy first outlined in Ernesto Laclau and Mouffe's *Hegemony and Socialist Strategy* in the 1980s, when they saw the route to this goal as being through the efforts of the various new social movements that had developed outside the standard political framework, citing as prominent examples

> the rise of the new feminism, the protest movements of ethnic, national and sexual minorities, the anti-institutional ecology struggles waged by marginalised layers of the population, the anti-nuclear movement, the atypical forms of social struggle in countries on the capitalist periphery.[21]

Left populism is intended to embrace the contemporary equivalents of such struggles, but whether it will have as much appeal to today's 'marginalised layers of the population' is a much more open question. Mouffe describes herself as being motivated by 'my conviction that it is urgent for the left to grasp the nature of the current conjuncture and the challenge represented by the "populist moment"'.[22] Right populism, however, claims to offer far quicker solutions to problematical issues such as immigration and multiculturalism (basically, stop it now in both cases and then start reversing it as quickly as possible), indicating the scale of the task that currently confronts the left in the struggle to win widespread support for a politics based on respect for, and fostering of, difference. It could be argued that 'the revolution of our time' that Laclau saw as emanating from the new social movements is actually occurring not on the left but on the right of the political spectrum.[23] If it is difference itself that is the main sticking point then right populism has a ready market for its beliefs, one very receptive to having its prejudices acknowledged and widely disseminated – and highly resistant to any argument that fails to do so. Once it gets underway as a force, right populism is not particularly interested in rational debate and resorts instead to inflammatory rhetoric, the intention being to polarise political positions such that it can exploit the tensions that result. Philosophical politics faces a particularly determined, as well as unscrupulous, adversary in this respect, one that is only too willing to descend to the level of mob tactics and threats in order to get its way. Large-scale public protests against immigration have become a regular feature on the European political scene and no country can consider itself to be immune to these; nationalism can be the most narrow-minded of beliefs, with almost no tolerance for the 'other'. Neither can left populism simply be a mirror image of this response in order to win the support of the disaffected, even if many on the left, sad to say, are also against immigration and multiculturalism, because that carries the danger of difference being suppressed and differends arising: a development that Lyotard is perpetually concerned to prevent. There ought to be a clear distinction between left and right on this issue if left-wing ideals are to be upheld: a noticeable difference in political style.

Mouffe nevertheless feels it is possible to put together a left populism that can take on the burgeoning right-wing version:

> The central argument of this book is that to intervene in the hegemonic crisis, it is necessary to establish a political frontier and that left populism, understood as a discursive strategy of construction of the political frontier between 'the people' and 'the oligarchy', constitutes, in the present conjuncture, the type of politics needed to recover and deepen democracy.[24]

For Mouffe it will be the struggle between right-wing and left-wing populism that will determine the future shape of our politics. She conceives of left-wing populism as 'informed by an anti-essentialist theoretical approach that asserts that society is always divided and discursively constructed through hegemonic practices'.[25] As a committed relativist, Lyotard would certainly agree with the need for an anti-essentialist ethos to politics: that attitude is engrained into poststructuralism and postmodernism alike, but whether populism would be the best way to conduct it would be more questionable, as it would go well beyond what he considers to be the remit of the little narrative. Mouffe's left populism really amounts to a secularised version of Marxism, assuming a mass movement with a set agenda stretching out into the future, but Lyotard's approach to politics is far more piecemeal than Mouffe envisages. Mouffe believes it is possible to win over right-wing populists by recognising their anger at their treatment by the neoliberal grand narrative, the currently dominant genre of economic discourse, and suggesting 'that, if a different language is made available, many people might experience their situation in a different way and join the progressive struggle'.[26] There is an assumption here that right-wing populists have been suffering from false consciousness and that if they could only be persuaded of this, then they would see the error of their ways and change sides. Theoretically anyway, this is always possible, but whether fascists would be open to the dialogue this would require is a moot point; as far as they are concerned it is the left that is suffering from false consciousness, not them. 'Might' involves a very significant leap of faith in this context. There is always the chance, too, that some of the left might be persuaded enough by the right's arguments to swap sides; you can never entirely rule that out either. Mouffe's optimism about the power of rational argument may well be misplaced in this regard (although it has to worry someone on the left like myself to make such an observation).

Lyotard emphasises what he calls the 'unharmonizable' in human affairs, and that means he will be inherently sceptical of the impact of mass movements, which have little patience with such phenomena.[27] From his Algerian experiences onwards, he is invariably more interested in the fate of individuals vulnerable to manipulation by the political machine (of whatever ideological disposition). Perhaps Mouffe does conceive of politics as being at least potentially harmonisable, however, and although her model of democracy as agonistic and pluralist would appear to allow for sharply differing political beliefs to exist within it, she insists on a certain amount of consensus as to what views can be campaigned for (although she would not see it as consensus, having an aversion to it as a political tactic). We may have adversaries in this system, but 'we have some common ground because we have a shared adhesion to the ethico-political principles of liberal democracy: liberty and equality. But we disagree concerning the meaning and implementation of those principles'.[28] There are of course many who would not have such a commitment to liberal democratic ideals. Neither communists nor fascists do, for example, meaning that they would have to be barred from the relevant political institutions, given that their goal would be to undermine their legitimacy and eradicate opposition, pluralism being anathema to both these groups. Somewhat paradoxically, perhaps, this indicates that even an agonistic, adversarial-based system of politics has limits as to what it will tolerate ideologically – agonism within limited parameters, it could be said. Although of course that brings with it the problem of who establishes what those parameters are – and who polices them too. It could be argued that Mouffe's insistence on the 'ethico-political principles of liberal democracy' would most likely result in a two-party system such as we already have in the UK, in that it would lock out extremists at either end of the political spectrum, with left populism and right populism swapping places in government in standard parliamentary manner: a democracy of the middle ground only. It is just such a restrictive system that the little narrative notion is set up to combat; as outlined by Mouffe it all looks a little bit too cosy, lacking the fluidity and flexibility that Lyotard is always seeking in politics.

While little narratives would have to feature at least a certain degree of consensus as well in order to pursue their objectives, they would be contained within the particular campaign they were waging and would not outlast it in the manner that left populism would want to. Everything would have to start all over again if a new campaign began to emerge, targeting a particular social issue or abuse; previous practice would be of no account. Ideology, such as it would be under a system of that nature, would be made up as the process went along, applicable to that particular campaign and that particular campaign only and not beholden to the two-party system. 'Here and now' would be the operative principle, and for Lyotard that is the only way of keeping authoritarian impulses at bay. Mouffe is a more conventional thinker than Lyotard in that regard, making assumptions that do not sound as if they would open out political life as much as she is hoping they would, and that could very well come to take on the character of grand narrative principles in time, 'shared adhesion' pointing that way.

Laclau was engaging with the concept of populism even before *Hegemony and Socialist Strategy. On Populist Reason*, for example,

is also concerned to make a case for the development of a populist hegemony of a left-wing character that could alter the political
landscape: what Laclau dubs a *'popular-democratic-interpellation'*.[29]
Laclau argues that '[p]opulism starts at the point where popular-dem-
ocratic elements are presented as an antagonistic option against the
ideology of the dominant bloc'.[30] Even though he concedes that this
will not necessarily turn out to be a revolutionary form of populism,
he thinks it can be made so if it can manage to 'precipitate a crisis in
the dominant ideological discourse . . . to the point where "the people" is completely unassimilable by any fraction of the power bloc'.[31]
Laclau assumes that the dominated class wanting to bring down the
dominant class would have to ensure the support of the people to
make their bid work, and that the people would come to realise the
extent of their antagonism to their rulers because of its articulation by
the said dominated class. As so often in the work of both Laclau and
Mouffe, however, the exact details of how we are to achieve this state
of affairs remains fairly vague. Phrases such as 'there is no socialism
without populism, and the highest forms of populism can only be
socialist' do not really take us very far either. The problem at the min-
ute is that the highest forms are not materialising and that the other
kind, based on a mean-spiritedness, are proving all too appealing to
'the people' across Western society. Apart from that, 'the people' is at
best a nebulous concept. Indeed, the pro-Brexit camp made a fetish
out of claiming to represent 'the will of the people', treating it as a
trump card in any debate about Brexit policy, even to the extent of
claiming that both parliament and the judiciary were to be seen as
the people's enemies (Slavoj Žižek's point that to disagree over what
constituted that 'will' was to prove to those claiming to represent 'the
people' that you could not be considered one of 'the people', neatly
summarises how difficult it can be to resist such loaded arguments).[32]
Any kind of populism will treat it in much the same way, using it to
suit its own ends to the point where it becomes ideologically overloaded, in which case one can see why little narratives would be well
advised to steer well clear of populist rhetoric. Populism almost inevitably contains the seeds of grand narrative.

Posthegemony and Populism

Laclau and Mouffe's hegemony-based view of politics, and the left
populism that could be constructed from this, has been challenged by
the call for a posthegemonic style of politics, as outlined by thinkers

like Jon Beasley-Murray, who offers an entirely different perspective on the notion of populism, preferring to speak of the 'multitude' instead of 'the people'. He rejects altogether the notion that cultural history is constructed by hegemony, of any variety, arguing that it is an outmoded, indeed all but mythical, concept: 'There is no hegemony and never has been. We live in cynical, posthegemonic times: nobody is very much persuaded by ideologies that once seemed fundamental to securing social order'.[33] Although Lyotard is not referenced by Beasley-Murray, this does sound very similar to the former's claim about the demise of grand narratives in *The Postmodern Condition*. Beasley-Murray goes on to argue that the belief in the need for hegemonic control is the unfortunate consequence of a comprehensive misreading of the nature of our historical development:

> [W]e have always lived in posthegemonic times: social order was never in fact secured through ideology . . . Social order is secured through habit and affect: through folding the constituent power of the multitude back on itself to produce the illusion of transcendence and sovereignty. It follows also that social change is never achieved through any putative counterhegemony.[34]

We are invited to regard hegemony, therefore, as little better than a 'fiction' and to recognise that there is no reason why we should allow ourselves to be taken in by it any longer; neither left- nor right-wing political theory has any justifiable claim to our loyalties.[35] The notion of a social contract, so important in political philosophy from at least the time of Thomas Hobbes onwards, is a critical aspect of that fiction for Beasley-Murray, so it is also to be treated with scepticism.[36] If there is domination in the world in the name of specific ideologies, as he agrees there still is, it is only because we allow there to be – and it is in our power to withdraw that support whenever we choose to.

As for left populism as a means of resisting such domination, Beasley-Murray argues that Laclau never really manages to establish a clear enough distinction between it and right populism, 'even to his own satisfaction'.[37] As just discussed above, Mouffe cannot be considered to have taken this much further in *For a Left Populism* either, certainly not in the sense of being able to offer guarantees that the multitude will be more attracted to the left kind than the right. The mass is always capable of being swayed either way if the rhetoric is powerful enough, and as even the most cursory glance at twentieth-century history would soon reveal, we should never underestimate the power of right-wing rhetoric (Hitler and Mussolini being the most obvious examples to cite, although there is a rogues' gallery of others to choose from). False consciousness is rarely a helpful way of explaining why this happens either, for all that so many left-wing thinkers continue to have recourse to it. Even Beasley-Murray, however, is light on specifics as to how the multitude operates:

> Social change, too, is achieved through habit and affect: through affirming the constituent power of the multitude. But change is not a matter of substituting one program for another. This book offers no blueprint, because the multitude betrays the best-laid plans.[38]

That does seem a rather sweeping statement, and we might wonder how we have managed to end up in a society where hegemony plays such a large role if its scope for operation is as limited as Beasley-Murray is suggesting. Whether the multitude always contrives to thwart the best-laid plans of the political class is a question worth asking as well (historical analysis hardly confirms this), as is whether some plans might be better than others in the political domain. The multitude can sound as threatening as a mob in that respect, potentially a negative force in cultural development, and little narratives would have to take issue with that possibility, given that 'habit and affect' would seem to have brought us both Trump and Brexit.

For Mark Purcell, too, left-wing thinking needs to move beyond the concept of hegemony in order to construct a new form of democracy that would give individuals greater freedom of action. Purcell's is a somewhat anarchistic form of democracy compared to Laclau and Mouffe's conception, which he feels is still too traditional and restrictive:

> Even though they advocate a politics of 'radical democracy', they do not leave open the possibility of democracy as a way of life beyond hegemony, or beyond the State. I think, instead, that we are capable of pursuing such a way of life, and even, if we are lucky, actually achieving it at times.[39]

In such a posthegemonic state populism would not be necessary, although posthegemony remains an extremely idealistic concept with significant barriers in the way of its realisation as political life is currently constituted. Social existence 'beyond the state' could turn out to be more like Hobbes's danger-ridden state of nature, where there is a 'warre of every man against every man', than a quasi-anarchist utopia.[40] If it is indeed just a fiction, hegemony is a fiction that seems to be very deeply embedded in the collective historical consciousness and as such cannot so easily be shed, especially when it comes to the institutions that represent and implement it, which, for better or worse, actually do command a considerable degree of popular support. The same points can also be raised about grand narrative; although, as I will go on to discuss next, we can at least speculate on how a political system constructed on posthegemonic lines might work.

Little Narratives and Liberal Democracy

Although there are similarities to be noted between Mouffe's left populism and Lyotard's political outlook, Lyotard instinctively shies away from the notion of mass action, being too iconoclastic a thinker to fit into such a pattern. He can only associate mass action with grand narratives and the hold they can exert over the population, thus a source of political problems rather than any solution to them: mass action implies a conformity that Lyotard could never accept. The little narrative remains his preferred method of challenging the dominant ideology, the most effective way as he sees it of preventing yet more grand narratives from developing and thus of protecting individuals from the oppressive power they can wield. Little narratives could be said to be intrinsically posthegemonic in character, not wanting to be tied to any particular party programme which would curb their room for manoeuvre and scope for adaptability and creativity, their orientation to the here and now. Applying the little narrative concept to the democratic system currently favoured in countries like the UK and the USA, where there are two main political parties contesting each election (Conservative and Labour, and Republican and Democrat respectively), would be an intriguing exercise and worth a thought experiment. In a two-party system politics tends to become very predictable, with each party having an ideological line that members pledge their allegiance to and which is supposed to hold, with certain variations, over time. Supporters therefore know broadly where they stand with the party of their choice. Although the parties themselves are broad coalitions, meaning that there are differences of opinion amongst their elected representatives and internal debates about policies, there is nevertheless an overall consensus about what principles the party stands for and about the need to maintain these to contest elections efficiently against one's adversaries. Loyalty to one's party is expected, and the notion of switching one's allegiance is very much frowned upon; it does happen, but relatively rarely and with little lasting effect on the existing system. Parties quickly close ranks after any such occurrence. Whereas it could be viewed as exhibiting a welcome sense of flexibility by the member actually making the change, demonstrating the 'capacity for discrimination' that Lyotard so prizes, it is instead reduced to being classified as either a betrayal or a conversion, depending on which side of the party divide the verdict comes from. It is not surprising that in such a political climate most elected representatives tend to suppress any opposition to particular party policies and remain within the fold; outside it they have little scope for meaningful action, especially if they choose to remain independent rather than join another existing party, as Change UK found in 2019 (the chances of them being re-elected as an independent are not all that high either, party loyalty tending to run very deep in the current system, especially when it comes to national elections). There is a tribal quality to this that a relativist thinker like Lyotard can only feel alienated by.

A Parliament constructed on the little narrative principle, however, would be much more fluid, in that its members would be free to join together to pursue particular causes without the restricting effect of party discipline; theoretically, at least, that concept and the notorious whipping procedures designed to keep everyone in line (as in the UK parliament's case) would disappear. (Although the whip is occasionally lifted to allow free votes in the existing system, it is only in very special circumstances and generally only after sustained pressure from a substantial number of representatives, with normal service resumed immediately afterwards.) Brexit provided a pointed lesson as to the limitations of the two-party system, with each party seemingly more committed to suppressing the little narrative groupings developing within it than trying to resolve a critical constitutional problem that demanded a far more adventurous approach that left notions of hegemony well behind. Party loyalty was placed above all other considerations, whereas in a little narrative based system it would have been a non-concern and the debate would have taken on a very different character, with less ideological baggage constraining individual members from following their inclinations (and Brexit presented multiple possible approaches to take). Any consensus that was reached under such a system would apply only to the issue at hand and would not commit members in the longer term; each issue that came to prominence would generate a different little narrative grouping, with the grand narrative of party kept at bay. If one could still speak of populism in such a context, then it would be a very fluid and dynamic phenomenon, constantly taking on new ideas and opinions and perpetually open to changes of direction and reassessment of positions. The danger with traditional forms of populism is that they can become very dogmatic indeed about their cause, to the point of being hostile to internal dissent and quashing it as quickly as they can, the tribal instinct taking over. Since the mass always counts more than the individual in such contexts, populism can easily become totalitarian in style, as the current right-wing version is proving yet again. Little narratives, on the other hand, are specifically designed to swerve away from such a condition, being temperamentally anti-totalitarian and opposed to centralisation of power.

As I indicated would be likely in such a thought experiment, there would be certain disadvantages to note to the concept of a little narrative based democracy. It would, for example, tend to be very much focused on the short term – in effect, as each issue arose – with less sense of an overall vision that could plan for the future. Government would be a far less stable entity than it is now envisaged (although from a Lyotardean perspective stability can also be interpreted as inflexibility). Most likely such a system would also be largely reactive in character, lacking the security that the two-party system offers to the electorate as to probable outcomes; party principles dictate a fairly narrow spectrum of possibilities in that respect, which voters come to expect and depend upon. It has to be admitted that the sheer predictability of two-party politics does exercise an appeal on a significant part of the general public, suggesting that their political choices are quite straightforward, requiring a minimum of analysis on the individual's part: if you do not like party A's policy, and feel strongly enough about it, then change over to party B, or vice-versa (voters may do that, even if elected representatives are not supposed to). Yet events like Brexit and the Trump presidency have shown up how illusory that sense of security really is, with both phenomena proving extremely divisive in the way that they overturned traditional political conventions and cynically cultivated the creation of differends (truth versus post-truth, fake news and alternative facts being one of the most notorious of these in the impact it is having on the public sphere).[41] The two-party system does not always guarantee political stability, therefore, or even clear outcomes. The little narrative option would encourage a much more thoughtful, philosophical – in Lyotard's sense of the term – approach to politics, one

24

in which issues rather than parties were the top priority. It would no longer be a case of politics as tribalism.

In other European countries there is often a wider range of parties involved in the political process, with the result that coalition governments are a more common feature there than in the UK, where they are the exception rather than the rule. This does allow for a greater degree of flexibility in putting together governments than the two-party system assumes, although it is not quite the little narrative model in that each party in the coalition is concerned to win concessions that keep its supporters happy and that do not affect its traditional ideological profile to any really significant extent. Loyalty is still a critical factor in the overall process (as is a wish for the power of office, a predictable effect of party politics), even if it is more diffuse in such a system, with a range of ideological positions being represented in smaller party groupings from left through centre to right. Individual members are still subject to constraints from within their own party that narrow their options. The flexibility is between the parties and how they agree to cooperate within a coalition, whereas little narratives are looking for that to apply right down to individual level, circumventing considerations of loyalty – except to one's conscience. Hegemony is therefore being maintained within the coalition set-up, whereas little narratives want to push past that to a posthegemonic state which offers greater freedom for individual politicians to follow the dictates of their conscience: the free vote principle as standard procedure, therefore, with whipping consigned to the past.

Another issue that would arise with a little narrative system is leadership. In the liberal democratic system leaders have a substantial degree of power (as in appointing cabinet ministers, for example) and can, to at least some extent, dictate government policy and parliamentarian tactics. Lyotard would seem to envisage a much looser system for little narratives, with no overall leaders and anyone free to put together a campaign and try to attract followers to see it through. Once the campaign was over then any nominal leadership that had applied during it would be expected to lapse. The point would be to prevent the emergence of charismatic leaders, with all the threat of authoritarianism and repression of dissent that comes along with such a development. Leadership in a little narrative system would have to be a far less formal, or powerful, position than it tends to be in the current party system and that would need some significant re-thinking of how we conduct politics. Given the trend towards strong leaders internationally (Trump having become a role model for far-right politicians) that is an activity that deserves encouragement. It is no accident that one-party systems traditionally favour the strong leader concept in that it makes opposition considerably harder to organise; dissent all too often ends up being interpreted as treason in such situations, especially when, as so often happens, the strong leader claims to be the authentic voice of the people. Little narrative, on the other hand, looks to create activists rather than leaders, predicating a far more radical form of democracy than recent political history in the West has seen: one that really does go right down to the grass roots. Lyotard's call for the concept of politician to be overhauled would be unlikely to include support for strong leaders, or any of the traditional styles of leadership for that matter. Inasmuch as we can speak of leadership in the case of little narrative, it would be a temporary position that would keep being passed on as campaigns evolved. The objective would be a more egalitarian form of politics which steered clear of the straitjacket of the two-party system, as well as avoiding the rise of personality-based politics.

Philosophers Against the System

As for the kind of politics philosophers should be engaging in as the political system is now constituted, Lyotard suggests that they should 'alternate between harassing the state and harassing capital'.[42] The point is to catch society's authorities and institutions off-guard by operating on a wide range of fronts in a freewheeling, non-party, non-doctrinaire manner that is hard to second-guess and thus defend against. To that end, Lyotard 's advice is that we should

> use laws and institutions against the abuses committed by entrepreneurs, organize tenants' associations, shopfloor struggles, ecological campaigns . . . And use the opposite argument, and the right to be an entrepreneur, when it is a matter of checkmating some dangerous state monopoly: set up pirate radio stations, invent unorthodox teaching methods (as at dear old Vincennes), try to unionize soldiers or prostitutes . . .[43]

Lyotard is well to the outside of both right- and left-wing orthodoxy in recommending such an apparently anarchic programme, deliberately playing games with doctrine by moving in and out of it as it suits his purpose, never allying himself with one ideological position for long enough to be regarded as a loyal supporter or to restrict his further actions. He studiously avoids tribal politics, preferring to

26

drift wherever his concerns might take him. It is all supremely tactical, using grand narratives to undermine grand narratives, without
putting forward yet another of your own which would make you
vulnerable to attack in turn. What it shows is that Lyotard is an anti-
doctrinaire, iconoclastic thinker, making it difficult to pin him down
as a political theorist. It is well to remember this as we work our way
through his oeuvre: Lyotard is always capable of surprising us by the
moves he makes, always the tactician concerned to wrong-foot the
ideologically committed and alter the character of debate.

Notes

1. Lyotard, *The Differend*, p. xiii.
2. Brecht, *The Resistible Rise of Arturo Ui*, p. 99.
3. Lyotard and Thébaud, *Just Gaming*, p. 55.
4. Lyotard, *The Differend*, p. 139.
5. Lyotard, 'A Podium Without a Podium: Television According to J.-F. Lyotard', in *Political Writings*, pp. 90–5 (p. 95).
6. Lyotard, *The Differend*, p. xi.
7. Lyotard, *The Postmodern Explained to Children*, p. 116.
8. Lyotard, *The Differend*, p. xiii.
9. Ibid., p. xiii.
10. Lyotard, 'Tomb of the Intellectual', in *Political Writings*, pp. 3–7 (p. 6).
11. Jones and Woodward, 'Setting the Scene', in *Acinemas*, pp. 3–9 (p. 7).
12. Jones, *Lyotard Reframed*, p. 12.
13. Lyotard, 'Rewriting Modernity', in *The Inhuman*, pp. 24–35 (p. 25).
14. Mouffe, *For a Left Populism*.
15. Lyotard, *Peregrinations*, p. 5.
16. Ibid., p. 27.
17. Lyotard, *Driftworks*, p. 91.
18. Lyotard, 'Nanterre, Here, Now', in *Political Writings*, pp. 46–59 (p. 57).
19. Fukuyama, *The End of History and the Last Man*.
20. Lyotard, 'Time Today', in *The Inhuman*, pp. 58–77 (p. 73).
21. Laclau and Mouffe, *Hegemony and Socialist Strategy*, p. 1.
22. Mouffe, *For a Left Populism*, p. 1.
23. See Laclau, *New Reflections on the Revolution of Our Time*.
24. Mouffe, *For a Left Populism*, p. 5.
25. Ibid., p. 10.
26. Ibid., p. 22.
27. Lyotard, 'Introduction: About the Human', in *The Inhuman*, pp. 1–7 (p. 4).
28. Mouffe, *The Democratic Paradox*, p. 102.

29. Laclau, *On Populist Reason*, p. 144.
30. Ibid., p. 173.
31. Ibid., p. 196.
32. See Žižek, *The Sublime Object of Ideology*.
33. Beasley-Murray, *Posthegemony*, p. ix.
34. Ibid., p. ix.
35. Ibid., p. 1.
36. See Hobbes, *Leviathan*.
37. Beasley-Murray, *Posthegemony*, p. 16.
38. Ibid., p. x.
39. Purcell, 'Democracy Beyond Hegemony', p. 298. For an argument against posthegemonic interpretations of Laclau and Mouffe, see Munck, 'Democracy Without Hegemony'. The various contributors to that issue of *Global Discourse*, 'Reflections on Post-Marxism: Laclau and Mouffe's Project of Radical Democracy in the Twenty-First Century', analyse both hegemony and posthegemony from a variety of angles.
40. Hobbes, *Leviathan*, p. 188.
41. I discuss the conflicts this is giving rise to in contemporary society in Sim, *Post-Truth, Scepticism and Power*.
42. Lyotard, 'Lessons in Paganism', in *The Lyotard Reader*, pp. 122–54 (p. 152).
43. Ibid., p. 152.

Chapter 2

Relativism and the Problem of Value Judgement

All sceptically inclined thinkers have to face up to the problems that relativism presents them with, in particular how to make and then defend
value judgements, an essential part of political life where choices are
constantly having to be made between competing courses of action
that can have dramatic effects on a nation's lifestyle and prospects.
Poststructuralist and postmodernist thinkers are regularly criticised
for evading this issue, a long-standing one in the history of scepticism
in Western philosophy. Unlike so many of his sceptical peers, however, Lyotard does not evade the problem. Throughout his career we
find him striving to reconcile relativism and scepticism so that value
judgements about ethical issues can be justified in some sense, even
from a relativist standpoint such as his own. The series of interviews
with Jean-Loup Thébaud that go to make up *Just Gaming* are cen-
trally concerned with this problem, as is Lyotard's contribution to the
'Heidegger Affair', *Heidegger and "the jews"*. In *Just Gaming* Lyotard
outlines a pragmatic approach to value judgement, and how this compares to the work of other pragmatist thinkers, such as Richard Rorty
(*Consequences of Pragmatism*, for example), will also be discussed
here. The concept of the pagan that Lyotard outlines in *Just Gaming*
emphasises the contingency of belief in general, a central theme of his
work and of his opposition to the grand narrative principle. It makes
an interesting comparison with the view of belief outlined in classical
scepticism by Sextus Empiricus, who opted out of belief altogether
when he realised it could never be properly philosophically grounded,
that all propositions implied an earlier one in what amounted to an
infinite regress.[1] It is a logical enough conclusion for a sceptic to make,
but from Lyotard's politically attuned perspective such a move would
be irresponsible. It would, apart from anything else, play right into the
hands of extremists, who are completely unconcerned by such philosophical niceties as the grounding of concepts and theories, feeling no
need whatsoever to subject their beliefs to scrutiny. Sextus Empiricus
thought that opting out of value judgement altogether was the best
answer to the claims of the dogmatists, whom he saw as his major

philosophical opponents, but one can hardly see that as a strategy likely to deter fascists, racists, or hard-line nationalists, all of whom are prominent players in the current political mix. They will simply go away and make whatever decision suits them in the sceptic's absence. Dogmatism is the most persistent of opponents, impervious to doubt, and a thinker like Lyotard is well aware that he has to come up with persuasive arguments and tactical moves to counter their claims that they, and they alone, are the ones to be trusted. His philosophical thought is geared towards application in the wider context of everyday life; it is never a mere metaphysical exercise.

Just Relativising

Lyotard is pressed hard by his interviewer, Jean-Loup Thébaud, in *Just Gaming* as to how value judgements can be justified within the relativist epistemological framework he is espousing and he comes up with some interesting responses that reveal his pragmatist leanings. When Thébaud suggests that his concept of paganism itself constitutes a criterion, Lyotard replies:

> I have a criterion (the absence of criteria) to classify various sorts of discourse here and there. I have a rudimentary notion of paganism, and indeed I rely upon it in deciding. But this operation of classification belongs to a language game that has nothing to do with prescriptions.[2]

The critical point for Lyotard is that judging should not involve preconceptions on the part of the judges, nor adherence to a set code of rules (how possible, or even desirable, this would be as the basis for a legal system will be considered later). Decisions have to be reached on the basis of a careful assessment of the circumstances prevailing in each individual case, every presiding judge's 'fine capacity for discrimination' coming to the fore. A rule-bound approach deploying prescriptions is one that Lyotard will never sanction, because it will reveal only the objectives of the grand narrative authorities who devised the prescriptions in the first place with the aim of strengthening their power base. Whoever draws up and implements the rules runs the system to their own advantage, rendering dissent difficult, whereas Lyotard is adamant that 'one cannot derive prescriptions from descriptions'.[3] It is worth mentioning in passing at this point that Lyotard's tendency to keep breaking up issues into components of various language games, which are taken to be self-contained entities in terms of their rules of operation, can be questioned. While it enables him to maintain his relativist stance, it is by no means always clear that descriptions of moral dilemmas and prescriptions as to how to deal with said dilemmas can, or should, be separated in this stark way. It can come across as an artificial resolution on Lyotard's part, a means of swerving round the issue in question. This is a recurrent problem with his philosophical method that I will keep returning to throughout the rest of this study; opponents simply would not see the separation between language games that he does – and needs in order to make his philosophical politics work.

Relying on individual judges to reach decisions without reference to a set legal code has the not insignificant drawback that it assumes a particularly open-minded kind of individual able to keep personal views, and particularly prejudices, at bay. With no criteria to go on, a point on which Lyotard insists, the result could well be wide variations in decisions on similar issues amongst the judging community – indeed, the procedure would seem to encourage just such an outcome. This is exactly what a rules-based, prescriptions-reliant system is designed to prevent occurring, or at least to keep to a minimum. The objective in the latter kind of set-up is to treat everyone equally or at least to be thought to be doing so, with the same set of rules applying to all cases rather than individually devised 'working hypotheses' that no one could know about beforehand (it has to be conceded that working hypotheses have an ad hoc quality to them that most legal systems would find problematic). Whether human beings are capable of being as dispassionate as Lyotard would require them to be when operating as judges, or as lacking in preconceptions – especially when it comes to ethical matters, which invariably arouse strong emotions – also has to be very doubtful. It would not be as apparent that everyone was receiving a fair hearing, or judgement at the end of it, under such a regimen, and consistency is generally taken to be an essential element of a legal system, particularly in liberal democracies. For Lyotard, however, fairness is more about being attentive to all the circumstances prevailing in each given instance and giving them due weight before coming to a decision, rather than assuming that criteria can hold unproblematically over time. This could be criticised as overly idealistic, although at least in principle it would seem to be an effective way of preventing grand narrative hegemony from establishing itself, given Lyotard's insistence that every case should start from a blank slate and be keenly attentive to the 'here and now'. In other words, social norms have to keep being reinvented (even if only in the sense of modified or expanded), although one assumes there would be a certain amount of continuity with prevailing ethical norms and codes at any stage of such a process. Judges are products of their culture and can hardly fail to draw on their knowledge of how this works, or what could be considered acceptable within it in moral terms. Axel Honneth's recognition theory, with its emphasis on the need for social relationships based on respect if moral conflicts are to be reduced, provides some pointers as to how we should expect such a system to function. It envisages a network of individuals reacting to and influencing the implementation of decisions to do with social justice, and it is the society's norms against which the decisions are to be measured rather than any overarching set of laws.[4] Judges would therefore be answerable to those norms and how they were perceived by their fellow citizens, with morality becoming largely a matter of personal relations instead of adherence to a supposedly absolute code. It is worth noting, however, that objections have been raised about the possibility of the overall social network becoming reactionary in character and thus highly resistant to change, which would run counter to Lyotard's political aims.

A further problem to be considered here is what happens when a judgement has to be made by a group or committee rather than by just one individual (as Lyotard's line of argument seems to imply is the model). At that point analyses could well clash and most probably would. The possibility of prejudices or preconceptions intruding on judgement would multiply under such a system, which would be an interesting test of Lyotard's pragmatism as one would assume some sort of criterion would be needed to decide between potentially different judgements. Having to operate without criteria at each stage in such a process would simply lead to the dreaded infinite regress. It is just such problems as the above that leave commentators such as Chris Rojek and Bryan S. Turner unconvinced that Lyotard offers us a workable system of justice: 'On pragmatic grounds Lyotard's philosophy of paganism and judging "without criteria" is a non-starter in contemporary culture'.[5] The notion of having 'to rethink constantly our responses to situations from first principles' does not at all appeal to them and it has to be said it is an objection that carries some weight – a society without rules would sound too anarchistic for most, and is clearly not consistent with historical precedent.[6] Whether systems serving the general public could achieve an acceptable level of operational efficiency under such circumstances has to be very open to question. As stated before, however, judges are operating within a cultural system of beliefs which will influence their decisions in ways that are understandable to others, even their critics; they are just as much a part of the social network, with its agreed norms and values, as any of their peers.

Judging Fascism

Heidegger and "the jews" brings the issue of value judgement into very sharp focus, with Lyotard unwilling to countenance the possibility that relativism offers any kind of escape route for figures like the Nazis. This is an ethical issue on the grand scale that cannot be sidestepped by reference to an infinite regress, and it is emphatically political rather than philosophical in its implications; philosophy has to be at the service of politics in Lyotard's scheme of things. Difference was plainly not being respected when it came to the Jewish population of Nazi Germany and the countries it invaded and occupied in the Second World War, and to Lyotard that was unforgivable, rendering Martin Heidegger's support for the Nazi regime a case of being complicit with the policies that led to the Holocaust. Recognition, in Honneth's sense of the term, was being withheld. Heidegger's public silence on this issue in the post-war period is to Lyotard an omission that cannot be allowed to pass without critical comment; ignoring the issue in this manner is not an option that Lyotard can be persuaded to condone. Heidegger is failing to bear witness to what had happened, the primary requirement of the philosopher in Lyotard's scheme of things: taking refuge in silence is not an acceptable tactic. Bearing witness in this case would mean recognising that the grand narrative one had been following was fatally flawed – as all grand narratives inevitably are in Lyotard's opinion. Nazism may be an extreme example, but grand narratives always have the capacity for development to extremes and it is up to philosophical politics to hold them to account if they start showing signs of this trait. Behind every instance of genocide will be found a grand narrative convinced it was in the right.

The wider point to be made in *Heidegger and "the jews"* is that societies through the ages all too frequently have been intolerant of minorities, refusing to accept their difference from the majority and discriminating against them on that basis. With depressing regularity we can see such minorities being turned into scapegoats to be blamed for any problems that the society could not resolve on its own (as immigrants were during Brexit, for example, and by the Trump presidency also). The majority were taking their grand narrative at face value, as the only true way of organising their society; whoever did not fit into that scheme had to be regarded with suspicion and minorities with different religions, languages, customs and ethnic heritage were, of course, highly vulnerable. Difference was to be regarded as the enemy, a threat to one's cultural identity. To Lyotard, all minorities who ended up being oppressed and intimidated in that manner could be referred to as 'jews', the victims of a differend where their legitimacy was manifestly not being acknowledged by the majority. Unless that tendency was addressed then similar injustices would continue to occur: one has only to think of the fate of the Rohingya in Myanmar in recent years to see how true that is – and, sadly, that is by no means an isolated case in the current world order, where scapegoating is a favourite tactic of unscrupulous politicians. *Heidegger and "the jews"* and its resonance for the contemporary geopolitical scene will be addressed in more detail in Chapter 6.

Judging Lyotard

Jacques Derrida has some interesting observations to make on the issue of value judgement in *Before the Law*, which opens with the provocative question: 'How to judge – Jean-François Lyotard?'.[7] The text was delivered at a conference specifically concerned with Lyotard's work on the topic of judgement and deals with it in the circuitous fashion so typical of Derrida's analyses, more concerned with what the concept of judging means, how we interpret it and whether our interpretation is justifiable, than in how to justify given judgements in given political situations. As is his wont, therefore, Derrida deliberately leaves the issue suspended; but what his reflections on it do succeed in bringing out is the complexity of what it means to judge and just how many factors have to be taken into account when doing so (and rarely are by most of us in everyday life). One of the most critical factors is whether any judgement we do make is in fact the product of a prejudgement:

> In its very form, the question 'How to judge?' seems at least to prejudge [*préjuger*] what it means to judge. The situation is that, since we know, or we *presuppose* what it means to judge, we ask ourselves only *how should we judge?* . . . In fact, as a title and as a result of its indeterminate,

suspended context, 'How to judge?' can have a radically critical effect on
the logic of the presupposition according to which we must know what
it means to judge before asking the question 'How to judge?'.[8]

The conclusion would seem to be that that we could never be in
a position to judge either with or without criteria, that there are
just too many barriers to frustrate us: a typically Derridean impasse,
where we do not know what to do next, only the difficulties that
beset any move we might want to make. Lyotard finds himself in
the same position, but does not leave the issue hanging as Derrida
does, deciding to press on without criteria when he is in such a situation and see what happens when working hypotheses are brought
to bear on it. That is not a move that would satisfy non-sceptical
philosophers, however, who would at best describe this as evasive:
an attempt to disguise that you do in reality have implicit criteria
which you are refusing to own up to. For Rojek and Turner, what it
means is that Lyotard is reducing judgement to 'a matter of feelings',
with all the uncertainty that would follow on from such a system.[9]
While that uncertainty has to be acknowledged, whether feelings can
ever be removed from ethical issues is something that does need to
be considered as well; when it comes to events like the Holocaust it
is hard to see how they could be and that will come across strongly
in *Heidegger and "the jews"*, where Lyotard's anger, even contempt,
for everything Nazism stands for is very evident. It is hard to see how
one could remain emotionally neutral about such issues – genocides
in general, in fact.

 While he is aware of the awkward position he is placing himself in
by swerving around the issue of criteria, Lyotard still feels the need to
establish conditions in which value judgements of some sort can be
made, otherwise those who choose to persecute 'the jews' will be able
to act with impunity. It is something of a tightrope walking exercise
and Derrida is right to point out that it does not provide the kind of
justification that we are generally looking for in the act of judgement
(if as he sees it, pointlessly); but Lyotard is also right that we have to
go through with this all the same if we want to address moral problems. A world without any judgement of those who persecute others
to further their own power is hardly thinkable; almost everyone's
personal security would be at risk were that allowed to happen. Asking ourselves if we can ever arrive at the stage of judging at all seems
a defeatist approach to such situations; that kind of thinking just
goes round in circles. Lyotard wants us to start from first principles,

whereas Derrida seems to be saying that we could never manage to establish first principles to proceed from. Questionable though it may often be (there is a glibness about his assertion that his criterion is to have no criteria when judging, even bad faith as many of his professional peers would probably see it), Lyotard's pragmatism keeps him politically engaged, constantly searching for non-prejudgemental solutions. Derrida, on the other hand, deliberately skirts around that condition: 'At bottom, the whole discourse on *différance*, on undecidability, etc., can also be considered as a means of keeping one's distance from judgement in all its forms (predicative, prescriptive; always decisive)'.[10] Lyotard would regard that as a dereliction of his philosophical duty: politics demands that decisions just have to be made if 'the jews' are going to be protected from the unscrupulous, and that is no mere intellectual game. Despite the many difficulties that relativism puts in his way, Lyotard will never keep his distance from judgement or refuse to take on that responsibility, therefore any judgement of him in turn has to take that into account as a very positive characteristic. Lyotard will not be one to stand on the sidelines when crimes against moral rights are being deliberated.

By making judgements Lyotard leaves himself open to assessment of his decisions from commentators who do operate with criteria, most likely derived from some grand narrative or other, so debate can always take place about the consequences. In many cases there could well be agreement as to the appropriateness of the decision made: for a start, few philosophers will argue the case for Holocaust denial. Derrida's distancing act from judgement makes clear the benefits of Lyotard's approach, showing us the two sides of relativism in effect.

Pragmatic Relativism

Lyotard's pragmatism is very focused on the issue at hand, in the moment that it occurs, and Richard Rorty's pragmatism displays similar characteristics, analysing each situation in terms of what the effects of competing courses of action would most likely turn out to be. James Williams also notes similarities between Lyotard and Rorty, but warns against identifying their concerns too closely given that Rorty is an ardent advocate of liberalism, a position Lyotard could never endorse (too closely identified with the Enlightenment project for one thing, so closer to grand narrative than he would ever want to be). For Williams, Lyotard espouses 'a nihilism that makes the claim that he is supporting or refining liberal democracy impossible to sustain', and we should be careful to note the differences between each thinker's political objectives as well as their use of irony.[11] These are fair points to make, but my interest here is to examine how they approach the issue of value judgements as confirmed relativists, without wishing to align them any more closely than that; on those grounds they are certainly worth comparing. Both are actively seeking solutions to moral issues, but being careful to keep prejudgements out of the exercise as much as they can (that is the ideal anyway). Pragmatism becomes a case of starting each time around from a clean slate and reacting to circumstances by devising working hypotheses to fit the developing situation. Anyone doing that as conscientiously as possible can feel reasonably confident in making value judgements, even in the absence of any universal law to cite as justification. As both of them demonstrate, relativism does not have to lead to a dead end like Derrida's.

Like Lyotard, Rorty avoids prescriptions and treats decision-making as an altogether practical affair, rather than feeling the need to justify it according to the dictates of some universal theory. He turns the tables on scepticism's critics by asking, rather disarmingly, why they feel the need to believe in absolutes such as 'truth', dismissing the notion that any foolproof theory about this concept is possible. In Rorty's view the search for such theories is pointless, not really a valid philosophical concern at all, because it has never yielded any positive results down through the ages, only a range of conflicting theories that still divide philosophers into opposing camps. Various philosophers have tried, and 'might have found something interesting to say about the essence of Truth. But in fact they haven't'.[12] What we ought to be doing in situations that require value judgements to be made is debating them, 'not in terms of categories or principles but in terms of the various concrete advantages and disadvantages' each proposed code of action has – a quasi-utilitarian approach, in effect, where the criteria emerge as the debate unfolds, with no preconceptions involved (in theory anyway).[13] Relativism is no bar to such a debate, which is seeking a consensus view of what would be the best thing to do given the particular circumstances that apply, rather than simply following the rules as laid down by tradition: as with Lyotard, the latter are to be avoided as prejudicial to an open-minded decision. Weighing advantages against disadvantages is explicit in Rorty, at least implicit in Lyotard, where we have to assume that concerns of that kind would run through the judge's mind (fuzzy logic uses a similar method in making decisions, working out a 'fuzzy weighted average from the information available' on the basis that truth is never as clear-cut as we tend to think it is, except in specialised formal systems like mathematics).[14]

Pragmatism always has to be open to the possibility of compromise when it is seeking to establish a solution to a debate, especially one involving a differend: being a relativist allows one considerable freedom of manoeuvre in that regard as you 'alternate between harassing the state and harassing capital'. Compromise becomes just one more move in an ongoing process, not the end of the road; each party can keep reassessing its position in response to unfolding events and adapting its tactics accordingly. It is not to be seen as a case of being untrustworthy or unreliable. Yet compromise is precisely what is becoming more and more difficult to achieve in the current political climate, where extremist ideologies are working so hard, and so often successfully, to dictate the terms of debate and to marginalise differends. Neither President Trump nor the Brexiteers are even remotely interested in compromise; to them, that is a sign of weakness rather than of democratic protocol, as would be the very notion of respecting differends. Political debate from their perspective is about humiliating and, if possible, silencing your opponent altogether, because any opposition at all is seen as unjustified; for Trump and the Brexiteers, little short of treasonous. It is that kind of dogmatism that Lyotard's pragmatism is taking on.

Conclusion

Relativism should not absolve one from having to make value judgements, and Lyotard maps out various ways of doing so without the need for any grand narrative prescriptions. He remains a relativist nevertheless, although one acutely conscious that some courses of action and ways of living are far preferable to others and that choices will always have to be made as events unfold around us. Political developments like fascism and shocking phenomena on the scale of the Holocaust demand that judgemental response; they cannot simply be ignored. He is open to criticism, as any relativist would be, when judging as if according to the promptings of a social conscience, given that this is then functioning as a criterion and relativism would appear to forbid such an assumption. Perhaps we have to acknowledge that there are at least some implicit assumptions in operation in Lyotard's thought that will point him towards adopting certain positions on key socio-political issues rather than others (that may well be the case with any of us). He is politically somewhere on the left, after all, even if keeping his distance from any particular party or theoretical position there after his early activist days, and he is very definitely against antisemitism and fascist ideology. All of this demonstrates that being a relativist is not for Lyotard a value-free condition and that he fully recognises the need to develop procedures to make, and then defend, the judgements he feels he must reach – to reveal what he is opposed to as much as anything else. Lyotard is always operating in this type of in-between situation, constantly having to invent ways of taking up positions without identifying with any grand narrative, of judging without expressing any specific ideological commitments. This is what thinking philosophical politics involves and no matter how awkward the project may prove to be, Lyotard will never be less than diligent in its pursuit. Judgements just have to be made if dogmatism and evil are going to be challenged.

Notes

1. Sextus Empiricus, *Outlines of Scepticism*.
2. Lyotard and Thébaud, *Just Gaming*, p. 18.
3. Ibid., p. 59.
4. See Honneth, *The Struggle for Recognition*.
5. Rojek and Turner, 'Introduction', in *The Politics of Jean-François Lyotard*, pp. 1–9 (pp. 3–4).
6. Ibid., p. 4.
7. Derrida, *Before the Law*, p. 3.
8. Ibid., p. 13.
9. Rojek and Turner, 'Introduction', in *The Politics of Jean-François Lyotard*, p. 3.
10. Derrida, *Before the Law*, p. 17.
11. Williams, *Lyotard and the Political*, p. 126.
12. Rorty, *Consequences of Pragmatism*, p. xiv.
13. Ibid., p. 168.
14. See Kosko, *Fuzzy Thinking*, p. 176.

Chapter 3

Lyotard and the Post-Marxist Turn

Over the course of the later twentieth century we can note a post-Marxist turn occurring in left-wing thought in Western Europe, and Lyotard is to be considered an important part of that process. It is not just a case of a few mavericks choosing to be contrary either; figures such as Lyotard are symptoms of a crisis within Marxism, a growing disenchantment on the left as to the validity of both its theory and practice, its historical record giving little sign that it really was the route to greater human freedom or an end to economic exploitation, as it had been promising from *The Communist Manifesto* onwards. The Soviet Union was proving a poor advertisement for what 'the forcible overthrow of all existing social conditions' that Marx had called for could actually lead to.[1] As a product of the post-war years, a time when the Communist Party was a significant force in French political life and Marxist theory very influential within the French intellectual community, it is not surprising that Lyotard felt the need to position himself against this tradition. Although he can be loosely categorised as a Marxist in his early career as a member of the Socialisme ou Barbarie group, then later as an activist in Pouvoir Ouvrier, Lyotard could be very critical of Marxism's authoritarian impulses, and the Stalinist period in Soviet history alone had made it very evident how deeply rooted these could be in the Marxist political class (Maoism was beginning to provide yet more evidence of the same by the 1950s). To be a science of society in the Soviet Union meant controlling all facets of that society's existence; the party's imprint was everywhere, a phenomenon no serious thinker on the left could fail to notice (even if many felt it was an acceptable part of communism's growth as a socio-political force given the scale of its ambitions and the hostility of the opposition it provoked). Lyotard's relationship with Marxism therefore constitutes one of the defining characteristics of his development as a thinker, marking a movement from ambivalence through to outright opposition as his career progressed. His antipathy towards universal theories sets in very early and never wavers.

40

The ambivalence towards Marxism is noticeable from Lyotard's Algerian writings of the 1950s for Socialisme ou Barbarie's journal, where he called into question the applicability of Marxist theory to the Algerian Revolution, arguing that it did not fit the situation prevailing there after the overthrow of French colonial rule. Given that Soviet communism was so influential in the burgeoning post-colonial movement of the post-war period, this analysis ran contrary to left-wing orthodoxy at the time, bringing out an iconoclastic strain in Lyotard's thought that would become steadily more pronounced. Then, after the 1968 *événements*, Lyotard, like many left-wing French intellectuals, turned against Marxism altogether, regarding it as badly out of step with the way culture was developing, to the extent of failing to recognise where truly revolutionary sentiments were emerging. Whereas cultural change demanded theoretical flexibility and creative tactical thinking, classical Marxism could only offer a rigidity of approach that was beginning to look seriously old-fashioned by the late 1960s, a relic of an outmoded worldview more concerned with form than substance. As Lyotard was to declare later in *Just Gaming*,

> [the] derivation of the political from the theoretical, in Plato or in Marx, for example, does not seem to hold for modern society, because the latter has an 'answer' of its own to the question. In fact, it has had this answer for quite some time.[2]

To Lyotard, Marxism was demonstrating that it was incapable of dealing with a phenomenon of the *événements'* magnitude and significance and that failing could not be excused or just ignored – as it certainly would not be by the *soixante-huitards*. Marxists simply had no 'answer' to a situation that did not meet their expectations, where theory and reality were not matching up. In the aftermath of 1968 *Libidinal Economy* marked a complete – and spectacularly bad-tempered – break with Marxism on Lyotard's part, and he was to continue his attack on universal theories in his most famous work, *The Postmodern Condition*, with its rejection of grand narratives in general. 'We no longer have recourse to' such theories or ideologies, he proclaimed, meaning that he did not anyway, and undermining the grand narrative ethos becomes a consuming concern of his writing, whatever area he is working in – from philosophy and politics through to the arts. Anti-authoritarianism can be considered Lyotard's default political setting.

The anti-authoritarian, anti-teleological bias of Lyotard's thought aligns him with many other thinkers in the post-Marxist movement such as Ernesto Laclau and Chantal Mouffe, although they retained a certain affection (as well as respect, if possibly somewhat on the grudging side) for the Marxist tradition that Lyotard plainly did not share. In a reply to their critics they claim, for example, that it is their intention to preserve 'the theoretical dignity' of Marxism, despite feeling the necessity of spelling out its 'limitations'.[3] Respect for Marx is signally missing from *Libidinal Economy*, which is instead openly insulting to Marx and his legacy, going out of its way to provoke anger on the left (which it clearly did, losing Lyotard many friends): 'Why, political intellectuals, do you *incline towards* the proletariat? In commiseration for what?', being representative of its general tone.[4] Despite the outburst of *Libidinal Economy*, however, Lyotard is never to lose his left-wing orientation, and it is not unreasonable to contextualise him within the post-Marxist turn. Post-Marxism is to be seen as a spectrum of beliefs rather than a set position. To classical Marxists, however, post-Marxism of any description equates to anti-Marxism, and Laclau and Mouffe's work is just as definable as that as Lyotard's is, despite the differences in their attitudes towards the Marxist tradition. For true believers any questioning at all of the Marxist canon is to be regarded as an attack on its integrity and therefore unacceptable; commitment has to be total, nothing less will suffice. Dialogue with post-Marxists cannot be countenanced, unless it is to point out the error of their ways and brand them as traitors to the cause – and classical Marxists were not slow in rising to the occasion to dismiss out of hand any suggestion of 'limitations', whatever its source.

The Rise of Post-Marxism

Marxism has always had its share of internal critics, but the movement as a whole – particularly the Communist Party – has traditionally been highly resistant to dissent, even of the mildest kind. Marx's works have come to take on an almost religious sense of authority for communists that precludes criticism. *Capital* is not just an intellectually rigorous analysis of a particular socio-economic system for this group (as even its many critics would be willing to concede), it is a received truth which will stand for all time, a science of society that can never be improved upon. It is the duty of followers to implement Marx's ideas, not to query them or raise doubts that could be turned to account by their ideological opponents, who would be on the lookout for any opportunities to sow discord within the movement (Marxism tends to promote something of a siege mentality).

Lyotard refers to that attitude in *Libidinal Economy* when he notes that: 'A Marxist political practice is an interpretation of a text, just as a social or Christian spiritual practice is the interpretation of a text. So much so that practices are themselves texts, insofar as they are interpretations'.[5] Text and practice have come to constitute a closed system in which each is taken to legitimate the other, creating an orthodoxy that demands obedience and forbids critique. This is a standard development in monotheisms, which naturally tend towards dogmatism, and Marx himself, Lyotard argues, exhibits a 'thoroughly religious love for a lost consubstantiality of men amongst themselves' that works to encourage the development of just such an orthodoxy.[6] Lyotard, however, refuses to be drawn into such a system, his assertion that 'this is precisely what we desire not to do here' setting the scene for a blistering attack on Marx's mystique.[7]

Jean-Paul Sartre was to make a similar complaint about the suppression of opposition in Marxist circles, when he noted that the tactic adopted by the French Communist Party in the 1940s when faced by such criticism was that 'the opponent is never answered; he is discredited; he belongs to the police, to the Intelligence Service; he's a fascist. As for proofs they are never given' (a tactic not unknown in liberal democracies as well, however).[8] Dissent was seen as little better than heresy in this milieu, where the party line was supposed to be followed without exception; classical Marxism has always emphasised solidarity over individual interpretation, being determined to present a united front to its many enemies. Sartre could not bring himself to support such a system:

> If it should be asked whether the writer, in order to reach the masses, should offer his services to the Communist Party, I answer no. The politics of Stalinist Communism is incompatible in France with the honest practice of the literary craft.[9]

Critical as he could be of communism and its methods, however, even Sartre felt compelled to try and come to an accommodation of some kind between his existentialist beliefs and Marxist thought, rather than to abandon Marxism altogether, an exercise he undertook at some length in his monumental *Critique of Dialectical Reason*. Lyotard, on the other hand, wants to stir up as much dissent as he can, on the grounds that 'invention is always born of dissension'.[10] Such a thinker is never going to feel at home within the collectivist ethos of Marxism; Lyotard is temperamentally always something of an outsider, even when it comes to movements he is sympathetic towards, such as postmodernism.

By the latter decades of the twentieth century, however, more internal critics were beginning to emerge within the Marxist movement, braving opposition to question some of its most basic theoretical principles. Western Marxism, as it came to be known, had begun this process by developing new ways of both reading and interpreting Marx, going back to the philosophical roots of his theories and opening up the possibility that Marx's principles were not infallible and perhaps needed to be refined, even altered, to reflect cultural change. As Perry Anderson put it, Western Marxism 'in effect constituted an entirely new intellectual configuration within the development of historical materialism'.[11] Practices were no longer to be seen as set in stone, and, at the very least, interpretation (which Marx had argued kept philosophers away from meaningful political engagement to change the world) was to be encouraged. This was a process that began as early as Georg Lukács' *History and Class Consciousness* in 1922, which, scandalously enough for the Soviet authorities concerned to establish control in the turbulent post-revolutionary period when it was meeting with both internal and external opposition, insisted that Marxism was more of an analytical method than a fixed body of principles that should never be diverged from by revolutionary movements. Lukács declared that '[o]rthodox Marxism . . . does not imply the uncritical acceptance of the results of Marx's investigations. It is not the "belief" in this or that thesis, nor the exegesis of a "sacred" book'; but that was precisely what Soviet communism was to go on and insist that it was.[12] To all intents and purposes, *Capital* was to become a sacred book to the communist establishment, and all analysis and study of Marx's thought from within that establishment was designed to prove its truth rather than to suggest that he may have been mistaken on occasion – or that he could be improved upon. Even such well-intentioned projects as Lukács's could not be condoned, to the detriment of communism's subsequent development. Lukács's fate acted as a warning to others that any critique at all of Marxist principles would turn you into an outsider, and in the Soviet system that was not just to put your reputation at risk but your personal safety also – as Stalin was to go on and prove with a vengeance, demonstrating everything that is wrong in the strong leader principle in the process (as in the notorious show trials that were conducted against supposedly dissident Party members in the 1930s). In the event Lukács was to recant fairly swiftly, adopting a more doctrinaire line in subsequent works and prospective internal critics no doubt took very careful note.

The Frankfurt School was to become even more critical of the Marxist world vision, with Theodor Adorno and Max Horkheimer's *Dialectic of Enlightenment* espousing a darkly pessimistic view of human nature and the historical process that sharply undercut Marxism's Enlightenment-derived optimism. For these thinkers, writing during the Second World War, what they are witnessing is 'the self-destruction of the Enlightenment', where the individual is being subordinated to the system on both sides of the ideological divide between capitalism and communism, 'wholly devalued in relation to the economic powers' wielded by the respective authorities.[13] They insist that 'the Enlightenment *must examine itself*, if men are not to be wholly betrayed' by the way culture is developing, but following the party line was hardly conducive to such detailed scrutiny of one's beliefs.[14] Adorno was to go on and reject the classical Marxist conception of the dialectic altogether in *Negative Dialectics*, arguing that there never could be any final synthesis of its elements, therefore no Marxist utopia to aim towards where all ideological contradictions would have been resolved by the triumph of proletarian ideals: 'a total philosophy is no longer to be hoped for', as he dismissed the notion.[15] The dialectic, in Adorno's iconoclastic interpretation, always remained open; the Hegelian-Marxist version was just too neat. There never was, nor could there be, a final synthesis of the dialectic's contradictory elements; it would remorselessly go on generating these, and to deny that was so was indeed to 'betray' humankind by misleading it as to the nature of material reality. It was a point that Lyotard was to echo, especially in his later works, which rejected the totalising imperative not just in Marxism but in ideologies in general. Lyotard saw all discourse, philosophy included, as a body of phrases which could always be added to, and phrases just kept coming on stream, no matter what barriers grand narratives put up to try and prevent this from happening: 'the "evidence" that we have to take on the burden of the linkages between thoughts and phrases does not mean that we can ever master them' (one might say the same thing of the internet, which reveals both the good and the bad points of the phrase linkage process).[16] There was no final statement, or interpretation, of anything, and he was tireless in pointing out what worked against the notion within discourse itself, such as figure, which formed a central theme in his published doctoral thesis *Discourse, Figure*. No system was to be considered exempt from the effect of the 'unharmonizable', a conclusion that was incompatible with how classical Marxists conceived of their science of society. What Lyotard wanted us to develop was the 'ability to tolerate the incommensurable' and that demands a very different style of political engagement indeed, although one that goes against the grain of how politics is standardly conducted in Western democracies, it must be said.[17] (One might wonder how such an idea would be received in a place like Northern Ireland, for example, where religious divisions are regarded as so incommensurable by both sides that the situation breaks down into sectarian violence on regular occasions, and at best is rarely more than an uneasy truce. A similar situation exists in India between Hindus and Muslims.)

The work of Barry Hindess and Paul Q. Hirst was also designed to undermine the Marxist conception of history, as they set about doing in *Pre-Capitalist Modes of Production* (1975) and *Mode of Production and Social Formation* (1977). Those two works challenged the notion that Marxism could be backdated onto earlier societies than Marx's own, as Marxism's theory that all history was the history of class struggle had insisted. Their argument was that this assumption was based on

> a misrecognition which engenders a cosy conflation between Marxist theoretical work and the historian's practice, a misrecognition which reduces Marxist theory to historical method and to a philosophy of history. Marxism is not a 'science of history' and Marxist theoretical work has no necessary connection with the practice of the historian.[18]

For Hindess and Hirst, Marxism applies only to a particular kind of social formation – that of rapidly developing industrialisation and the factory system from the nineteenth century onwards (Jean Baudrillard was to reach a similar conclusion). Even there, the knowledge economy that Lyotard was analysing in *The Postmodern Condition* was already eclipsing that formation, revealing Marxism's limitations as a universal theory: events were passing it by, both politically and technologically. The precariat that has developed out of this last phase further undermines Marxist theory, since, as Guy Standing has pointed out, in no way can it be considered a proletariat in the traditional Marxist sense of the concept, with its members standing in an identical relationship to the mode of production. There is simply not the sense of unity or shared experience amongst such a socially diverse group of individuals that could qualify as a Marxist-style class consciousness and provide the impetus for an anti-capitalist revolution; just too much difference getting in the way of the development of solidarity.[19] The precariat constitutes an inherently unharmonisable grouping, meaning that Marxist categories such as class, one of the most crucial in Marxist thought, are therefore failing the test of universality in the contemporary world: theory and reality out of step yet again. The very character of the knowledge economy is inimical to the notion of solidarity; it is far too fragmented and changeable for that, as well as far too amorphous to be vulnerable to challenge in traditional industrial relations terms – trade unionism does not flourish very well in such a setting and has been declining sharply in the West for years in consequence. Marxism is not really set up for a culture where 'move fast and break things' has become the preferred business model.

The precariat would seem to offer an opportunity to put into practice Lyotard's recommendation to 'alternate between harassing the state and harassing capital'. It would be a case of fighting on various fronts, in often contradictory ways (all the more to confuse your opponents), to subvert the dominant ideology. As with classical Marxist theory, it might require activists and agitators to start the process rolling, but Lyotard's suggested tactics do circumvent the problem of a lack of class consciousness. New tactics are certainly needed in a world where theorists have been announcing the death of the working class for some time now, a situation which capitalism has been exploiting to its considerable advantage through globalisation and neoliberalism.[20] Marxist theory has never really accommodated itself to the new world order of the knowledge and information economy.

Baudrillard went on to mock Marxism's obsession with production, especially its belief that this could ever provide the basis of human liberation, in *The Mirror of Production*: 'Can the quantitative development of productive forces lead to a revolution of social relations? Revolutionary hope is based "objectively" and hopelessly on this claim'.[21] In Baudrillard's interpretation, the obsession simply succeeded in enslaving humankind even more so than within the capitalist system it sought to displace, subsuming workers within the needs of the production process. Baudrillard's analysis has interesting echoes of Lyotard's mocking references to Marx's writing practices, with new material constantly being produced for *Capital* in what was almost a parody of the manufacturing system of the nineteenth century: 'a chapter becoming a book, a section a chapter, a paragraph a section'.[22] The idea that more is better is rejected by both thinkers, who see it as one of the most reprehensible beliefs in the Marxist scheme of things. No amount of grandiose Five-Year Plans on the Soviet model could succeed in making quantity equal quality. Yet despite the Soviet experience China continues to adhere to the production obsession, in this case, ironically enough, mass manufacturing goods for the Western market – often luxury ones at that, including expensive technological products. Its economy is now almost entirely based on this principle, which in its own way represents something of a turn from Marxist orthodoxy: this was hardly what Marx could have envisaged as the dictatorship of the proletariat, more a case of propping up capitalism. The old accusation bandied around by militants during the Cultural Revolution about certain Chinese Communist Party members being 'capitalist running dogs' now seems quite apt.

Not all Western Marxists set out to undermine the Marxist scheme; Louis Althusser, whose work was to be very influential on left-wing thought in the 1960s and 70s, sought to restore Marx's authority by insisting that if he was read properly, with due care and attention to the detail of his arguments against capitalist ideology, then the validity of Marx's thought would become apparent:

> Of course, we have all read, and all do read *Capital*. For almost a century, we have been able to read it every day, transparently, in the dramas and dreams of our history, in its disputes and conflicts, in the defeats and victories of the workers' movement which is our only hope and our destiny . . . But some day it is essential to read *Capital* to the letter. To read the text itself, complete, all four volumes, line by line, to return ten times to the first chapters . . .[23]

Althusser would seem to be suggesting that misreading and misinterpretation are the sins of much Western Marxist thought, an assessment to be contemptuously dismissed by Lyotard in *Libidinal Economy*: 'We no longer want to correct Marx, to reread him or to read him in the sense that the little Althusserians would like us to "read *Capital*": to interpret it according to "its truth"'.[24] The implication of Althusser's theories was that Marxism would still work if only it was interpreted correctly, line by line, read over and over again to ensure complete understanding, in which case it was not inevitably bound to turn out the way it had: it was his readers, not Marx's writings, that were at fault (religions often make the same claim for their sacred books; more intense Bible study will resolve any doubts that may have crept into your mind about the truth of Christianity, etc.). Thinkers like Lyotard, however, were not willing to give the latter the benefit of the doubt, seeing the blame to lie in Marxist theory if things went wrong, not in those seeking its essence or trying to implement it. Once again the quasi-religious nature of Marxist belief declares itself; the onus was on the believer to conform to what the theory said, 'confusing what they see with universal truth, and regressing', in Adorno's characteristically unsympathetic assessment.[25] For those who begin to have doubts about Marxism's contemporary relevance, its cult-like status becomes hard to ignore. The faithful are expected to obey, not to question the theory's principles; the latter could only be regarded as apostasy. What had started out as a movement dedicated to emancipating humankind had turned into its opposite, one that was repressive and policed individual thought and action very severely: hardly what the Enlightenment had set out to encourage.

Laclau and Mouffe's *Hegemony and Socialist Strategy* chose to challenge Marxism's pretensions to universal validity through a closely argued analysis of the role played by the concept of hegemony over the course of Marxism's history. The point of deploying hegemony, from Antonio Gramsci's work onwards, had been to protect the reputation of Marxist theory, in a bid to keep dissent at bay on the left and so maintain an ideological solidarity in the political arena.[26] If Marxism was not reaching its planned objectives then bourgeois hegemony was to blame, managing to maintain enough support to delay Marxism's predictions. Looking at it from a Lyotardean perspective, however, it could be said that, in effect, bourgeois hegemony was functioning much like a figure within Marxist discourse, preventing it from operating as expected; and to Lyotard, every discourse had its figure to contend with. Why bourgeois hegemony has continued to be popular, despite its obvious flaws and injustices (apparent not just to Marxists), is a problem that has taxed the classical Marxist establishment down through the years. The Gramscian line was that the populace had been lured into a state of false consciousness such that it could not recognise where its real class interests lay, being persuaded instead to adopt the values of the ruling bourgeoisie as its own. Generations of classical Marxist theorists subsequently bought into that argument to explain why communism had failed to have greater success in political terms throughout the West (Althusser being one of the most notable to develop the argument with his concept of the

Ideological State Apparatuses serving to explain the tenacity of false consciousness).[27] For Laclau and Mouffe, what this meant was that classical Marxism was dependent on a tradition of excuses, putting its integrity as a theory seriously at risk. It required constant tweaking to be able to claim any credibility at all as successive economic crises and wars failed to topple bourgeois culture. In scientific terms of reference, Marxism was by the late twentieth century a failing paradigm, and the authors of *Hegemony and Socialist Strategy* no longer felt inclined to help prop it up.

Understandable though such excuses might have been in the volatile climate of the post-First World War period, when communism was struggling to establish a political foothold in Europe, the effect had been to entrench authoritarian attitudes within the movement, which became particularly obvious during the Stalinist period in Soviet history. Stalinism remains a very considerable problem for the left, even at this far remove from its heyday: a permanent scar on the Marxist project that can always be used by its opponents to question its ethics. The question of whether Marxism encourages a Stalinist system cannot always be avoided, as Adorno's critique of its totalising imperative makes very clear. In Adorno's reading that imperative is firmly embedded in Marx's development of the dialectic, and as such will pose a threat to any communist project. Marxism posits an end and a route to that end, making it intolerant of any scepticism about its interpretation of history; an authoritarian party and a strong leader enforce this. For Adorno that means totalitarianism is endemic to Marxism, in which case Stalinism is no mere aberration but instead a major contributor to what he and Horkheimer bemoaned as '[t]he fallen nature of modern man'.[28] That is an uncomfortable conclusion for the left to live with; the dark side of Marx's 'thoroughly religious love for a lost consubstantiality of men amongst themselves'. Consubstantiality would appear to come at a considerable cost – freedom of thought has to go for a start.

Jacques Derrida gives us one of the most subtle and suggestive forms of post-Marxism in *Specters of Marx*. Marx is conceived of here as a spectral presence in world thought, a part of our history that we can never entirely escape from:

> It will always be a fault not to read and reread and discuss Marx . . .
> We all live in a world, some would say a culture, that still bears, at an
> incalculable depth, the mark of this inheritance, whether in a directly
> visible fashion or not.[29]

Marx, in other words, cannot be forgotten: but neither, crucially, can Stalin or the worst excesses of the Soviet system (or the Maoist). As a social analyst Marx can still inspire left-wing thought, but on the political side he leaves behind a much more problematic legacy: a 'hauntology' as Derrida puts it, rather than a fully worked-out ontology for a new society.[30] What starts out sounding like Althusser and his plea for a closer reading of Marx's texts soon diverges in intent. We know where Marx's theories have gone wrong rather than where they have gone right – not much of an advertisement for a supposedly universal theory. Marx's appropriation in the cause of totalitarian regimes such as the Soviet or the Maoist cannot simply be passed over. It is just such a legacy that Lyotard would seem to want to expunge from left politics – certainly from his 'philosophical politics', with its explicitly non-partisan bias. Even a spectral Marx is more than Lyotard would be prepared to countenance, as *Libidinal Economy* makes abundantly clear. True, Marx cannot just be forgotten, any more than Nazism can with respect to Heidegger, but that does not mean his objectives are worth pursuing any longer. The game is up for Marx as far as Lyotard is concerned and he feels under no obligation to be respectful in asserting his opposition. He simply feels irritated that a theory that 'was no longer anything but a screen of words thrown over real *différends*' is still drawing attention on the left as if its aims were in any realistic way recoverable.[31]

Derrida makes a point that most post-Marxists would be happy to agree with, however, and that is that Marx can be, and should be, interpreted in a multiplicity of ways:

> It will always be a fault not to read and reread and discuss Marx . . . There will be no future without this. Not without Marx, no future without Marx, without the memory and the inheritance of Marx: in any case of a certain Marx, of his genius, of at least one of his spirits. For this will be our hypothesis or rather our bias: *there is more than one of them, there must be more than one of them.*[32]

While this would be self-evident to post-Marxists, who are entirely open to Marx being constantly re-evaluated according to the dictates of cultural change (class, for example, is a very different phenomenon now than it was in Marx's day, a factor which surely ought to be taken into account), it would be all but heretical to classical Marxists. For the latter, Marx's message should be the same for all: without that, its authority dissipates and it becomes just one more theory competing for our attention in a very crowded marketplace. If Marxism is to cease being a universal theory, with a clearly identifiable set of principles and goals being passed on from generation to generation, then its value as a basis for social revolution can only decline very sharply. A postmodernised Marx would be beyond the pale; his work is supposed to be above theoretical trends, a science rather than a mere theory that can be superseded by others in the manner of a paradigm shift.[33] One can hardly see theorists like Althusser agreeing with that. Post-Marxism and anti-Marxism are therefore interchangeable terms from a communist perspective, which will always emphasise collective solidarity over the threat of conflicting multiple interpretations and the rise of factionalism within the movement (even if, ironically enough, factionalism is rife on the left in general, with splits over points of doctrine being all too common occurrences). Solidarity stifles the creative impulse within theoretical enquiry and quite deliberately so as far as the party leadership is concerned. Marxist theoreticians are not encouraged to think outside the box; the theory has to be correct no matter what events may appear to be telling us, thus the continued recourse to the concept of hegemony by the classical Marxist establishment to explain the bourgeoisie's unexpectedly stubborn dominance. From that position it is reality that is in need of reinterpreting, not Marxist doctrine. Communism's time will eventually come: a mere delay in its predictions should not be cause for alarm.

In *Ghostly Matters*, Avery Gordon, using a broadly Marxist approach, follows on from Derrida's notion of haunting as an insistent reminder that we cannot escape from our past, agreeing that it continues to shape our culture in subtle ways that we must learn to come to terms with. The degree of influence we should allow that haunting to have over us is, however, the critical point at issue. Both Derrida and Gordon argue for it as something that we cannot avoid: 'a constituent element of modern social life', as Gordon puts it, a reminder of unfinished business in our culture that calls for 'something-to-be-done' to correct past wrongs.[34] For Lyotard, however, this would be allowing the past to have too much control over us, effectively a case of being haunted by the ghost of grand narrative. He would agree with the need for 'something-to-be-done', but it would depend on the framework in which it took place: anything at all Marxist would not be acceptable.

Algeria: The Limits of Marxist Thought

Lyotard had taught in Algeria in the early 1950s, and his experience there led to him being appointed as the main commentator on Algerian affairs for the *Socialisme ou Barbarie* journal, an activity he kept up for eight years. This was at a particularly critical point in Algerian history, with the revolution against French rule gaining momentum and creating deep divisions within French society. Although in favour of the revolution (even if opinion was divided about it in the Socialisme ou Barbarie group itself, as it was about Marxist orthodoxy too), and an opponent of French colonialism, Lyotard was not convinced that the socialistic solution offered by the revolutionary forces of the FLN was the answer to Algeria's problems. As a predominantly peasant society, Algeria lacked most of the prerequisites for a social revolution that Marxist theory believed had to be in place to ensure a victorious outcome, and Lyotard's assessment of the situation reflected that:

> The problem of helping Algerians to live is conceived and solved in terms of an individual or a small collectivity, a village, a family, a quarter. No consciousness can span the whole of society so as to pose the question of what that society is for itself.[35]

Views like this put Lyotard severely at odds with classical Marxist thought, which firmly believed that Marxism was a theory to fit all such eventualities: Marxism's perspective was global, whereas Lyotard's was showing greater sympathy with the local. Ideologically, Lyotard was already beginning to drift away from Marxism and his scepticism regarding its totalising pretensions was to become progressively more pronounced over the next couple of decades. This was especially the case after the watershed of 1968 and what he and many of his contemporaries saw as an act of unforgivable bad faith on the part of the French Communist Party, which had supported the De Gaulle government against the strikers and student revolutionaries who had taken to the streets in an attempt to bring the government down. His antipathy to grand narratives was well entrenched in both his political and philosophical outlook.

Already in the Algerian writings, we can note Lyotard leaning towards the little narrative line of thought and thereby rejecting the authoritarian imperative so common to grand narratives – Marxism above all, with its refusal to countenance any significant deviation from the party line. Again the importance of the local was being emphasised over the global, with Lyotard pointing out that:

> [t]he unemployed person wants work: the woman wants bread for her son; the combatant wants to be honored for having fought; the student wants books and professors; the worker wants a salary; the peasant wants seeds; the shopkeeper wants to restart business.[36]

Just to complicate the matter further, as Lyotard rightly notes there was little in the way of a proletariat in such an underdeveloped nation as Algeria, nor a particularly powerful bourgeoisie either, making it a poor candidate for revolutionary success compared to Western Europe, which had been the focus of Marx's researches (although, to be fair, Chinese communism had managed to adapt Marxism to a predominantly peasant-based society, if with a considerable amount of difficulty that went on for many years). To Lyotard, this meant that Algeria under the FLN was on the way to being 'a new class society under the control of a bureaucratic military leadership', and the country's subsequent history tends to bear out his analysis.[37] Neither was Algeria the only example of such a development, of course, but that was not a message that most communist supporters wanted to hear at the time in the aftermath of the overthrow of French colonial rule. Even at this early stage in his career Lyotard was laying himself open to the charge of being anti-Marxist, unafraid to challenge theoretical orthodoxy by pointing out what to him were the limits of Marxist thought: 'When concepts or schemas are refuted by historical reality over a period of forty years, the task of revolutionaries is to discard them without remorse and to replace them with others that make an effective struggle possible'.[38] He describes his own position at the time with regard to Marxism as 'hopelessly contradictory' and he will never be one to follow the party line unquestioningly.[39] The notion of a philosophical politics is a logical development of that trait, one that does not involve the ideological baggage of a universal theory and is free to seek out new 'working hypotheses' to test in an empirical fashion. For Lyotard, the role of the philosopher is to be like that of figure within discourse, preventing grand narratives from claiming total control, pointing out where systems lack credibility – the very opposite of what intellectuals do, Marxist or otherwise. Philosophers were there to make life awkward for the ruling authorities, rather in the manner of guerrilla warfare: a symbol of unharmonisability to inspire others to reject the conformity that those authorities demanded. Above all else, philosophers were not to be ideologues; Algeria was a lesson to Lyotard that to adopt the latter character could only lead him into contradiction. Move away from Marxism, however, and that contradiction ceased to be an issue.

Libidinal Economy: *Marx and Desire*

Libidinal Economy was described by Lyotard as 'my evil book, the book of evilness that everyone writing and thinking is tempted to do' and it certainly makes no concessions to left-wing sensibility (perhaps we all have an 'evil book' within us, a point I will be returning to).[40] Marx is pilloried mercilessly in the text and comes across as a less than systematic thinker, someone continually adding to his researches as if never quite satisfied with the depth of evidence he was providing for his views; the British Library just went on yielding more material for him to process, meaning that *Capital*'s publication date had to keep being delayed. On the plus side, this does indicate a thinker concerned to answer all possible objections to his theories, and communists have accepted it in that spirit; since his death, *Capital* has been expanded to four volumes to demonstrate Marx's industriousness on that score. What it suggests to Lyotard, however, is that there is no final moment of synthesis in Marx's writings, an ironic point to make about a theory aiming for universal applicability and picturing itself to be the ultimate science of society, the one with all the answers. One of the things that militates against universality is desire and Lyotard argues that Marxism can be challenged on those grounds, sarcastically remarking that 'we wonder what there is of libido in Marx'.[41] Desire is working away within human rationality in a way that undermines grand narratives like Marxism (very much a product of Enlightenment rationalism in its optimistic outlook on humanity's future). Reason, in other words, is never fully in control of any human project, which is always going to be vulnerable to the unpredictable workings of desire, with Lyotard drawing freely on Freud's line of thought on the issue (*Discourse, Figure* having firmly established the latter's influence on him). The dissection of the human body which is described in *Libidinal Economy*'s early stages makes that point in a particularly graphic way. Desire is not there to be found in any of the body's parts, no matter how much you break it down, but it will nevertheless make its presence vividly felt when that body is out living in the world, functioning according to a libidinal economy. That economy is yet another unpredictable and subversive element working against the system, as figure is in discourse. Lyotard speaks of 'libidinal economy's deafness to the rules of composition, to the hierarchy of the organism'.[42]

Systems in general, including, crucially enough for Lyotard, political systems, can never be made 100 per cent effective; they will always be vulnerable to the effect of such phenomena as desire, figure, or the event – which is to say they are intrinsically unharmonisable, regardless of what grand narrative thinkers would like to believe. To pretend otherwise, as Marxism does in its quest for a perfectly ordered, utopian society where economic exploitation is a thing of the past and the dictatorship of the proletariat has been fully achieved, is delusional. The world will always turn out to be messier, much messier, than theory assumes it to be, and desire will be a critical factor in keeping it that way: contradictions will continue to arise and to resist synthesis. Lyotard is adamant that we must bear that knowledge in mind at all times, in order not to be taken in by the claims of grand narrative. *Libidinal Economy* sets out to make that point in such a way as to communicate Lyotard's despair that a grand narrative like Marxism can still find defenders, noting how he had 'the goal of inscribing the passage of intensities directly in the prose itself without any mediation at all. The project was quite naive and a little compulsive'.[43] It is all the more powerful for its intensity and compulsiveness, however, and we are certainly left in no doubt as to the depth of Lyotard's disillusionment with the Marxist movement. The text has to remain one of the most revealing works of theory (one is tempted to say anti-theory) from what must have seemed to someone so politicised as Lyotard to be a very dark period indeed in French political life. He was saying what many on the left were probably thinking but were too afraid to admit publicly.

One of the most provocative suggestions that *Libidinal Economy* has to make regarding Marx is that we should 'treat him as a work of art'.[44] That would mean dismissing his claims to have devised the ultimate science of society and to read him in a far more irreverent manner. Marx would then become more like a novelist than a prophet, someone whose work could be raided for ideas, to be used however the individual reader thought fit, with no concern about respecting their supposed theoretical purity: 'We must come to take Marx as if he were a writer, an author full of affects, take his text as a madness and not as a theory'.[45] To treat Marx's oeuvre and legacy in that way is to move well beyond classical Marxism, which is being stripped of its authority and prestige by such a thoroughgoing re-categorisation:

'mad Marx' hardly sounds like the most promising candidate for the post of revolutionary icon. Lyotard's Marx would give rise to multiple, individually centred interpretations of his work; but there is no suggestion that social or political theory would have much, if anything, to gain from the process. Marx could be taken or left, in the manner that any novelist could; engaging with him is not to be seen as a necessary rite of passage to make sense of one's world. No hauntology applies in this case; Marx is no longer holy writ, nor even the ghost of it. He is there to be experimented with, or played with, simply one more text amongst many competing for our attention. It is a markedly less respectful view of Marx's legacy than we find in Derrida; Lyotard would be quite happy were we to neglect that legacy altogether and get on with politics untrammelled by it.

A more measured argument against Marxism can be found in *The Differend*, where Lyotard considers what might be left of the theory after its pretensions to being a grand narrative have been undermined: 'Marxism has not come to an end, but how does it continue?'.[46] Lyotard suggests that Marxism is a response to a wrong done to certain sections of society, which 'is expressed through the silence of feeling, through suffering', and 'the silent feeling that signals a differend remains to be listened to. Responsibility to thought requires it. This is the way in which Marxism has not come to an end, as the feeling of the differend'.[47] Even if fault can be found with Marxism's solution to the differend (a confusion of genres in Lyotard's opinion), the differend itself remains and is to be respected. Marx had identified a social wrong that was calling out to be corrected, and each generation faces its own challenge in that regard. If nothing else, he provides us with an example of what we ought to be looking for as socio-political theorists and activists – the critical differends that our system of belief is trying to hide because they benefit those in power. That is, however, a far cry from being the creator of a definitive science of society that tells us how to remake the world after 'the forcible overthrow of all existing social conditions'. Marx might inspire us to stand up to our society's social evils, but not direct us on how we should address them; that is something we have to work out on our own, as each generation must in response to a continually changing cultural landscape. That kind of legacy Lyotard could probably accept, one that provides hints rather than methods or specific programmes of action. Provocatively enough, it is Marx's feelings that Lyotard wants to retain, not his monumental theoretical researches or ideological critique. Those feelings can still inspire us, as Lyotard implies, but where they take us has to be our decision, not classical Marxism's.

'A Memorial of Marxism' offers a much more personal take on Lyotard's turn away from Marxism, recounting the story of his resignation from the Pouvoir Ouvrier movement in 1966 and the rift this opened up with his former colleagues there, particularly the historian Pierre Souyri. In Lyotard's view it meant that there was now a differend between them:

> Our *différend* [form used in this translation] was without remedy from the moment that one of us contested or even suspected Marxism's ability to express the changes of the contemporary world. We no longer shared a common language in which we could explain ourselves or even express our disagreements.[48]

Looking back at Marxism's twentieth-century history, what Lyotard sees is the systematic failure of Marxist predictions in the face of capitalism's resilience, as in its ability to withstand world wars and economic depressions, and wonders whether this signals 'the failure of a way of thinking'.[49] In other words, there is a deficit between the theory and reality that can no longer be ignored, classical Marxists notwithstanding: Laclau and Mouffe will reach a similar conclusion. Lyotard's argument is that the deficit cannot be debated either within Marxist circles or outside, because Marxist theory cannot admit the failure of any of its principles. There is no language in which someone like Lyotard can debate with someone like Souyri: 'How could the means of expression known as Marxism put itself into play and debate about itself as though it were just one content among others?'.[50] It is akin to the stand-off that would arise if an atheist and a believer were to clash over the topic of the existence of God; what for one party needs proof, for the other needs none at all, being self-evidently true. For followers like Souyri Marxism constitutes an unalterable truth, a grand narrative rather than just one more little narrative striving to find support in the political arena. Marxists cannot see history as anything but the history of class struggle, because that is the very basis of Marxist theory. Therefore everything that happens has to conform to that principle. It is not something up for debate; Marx's writings provide the necessary proof of the proposition for Souyri et al. To deviate from that line of thinking is instantly to become a class enemy. Lyotard's position, however, is that this is a reductive view of history, drastically underestimating its complexity: 'The roles of the protagonists of history are not played out in a single genre of discourse'.[51] Marxism cannot accept that, since it considers itself to be the only valid genre of discourse, the one which, as Lyotard put it, 'claimed to be able to transcribe all genres' – a claim that no theory could ever be justified in making.[52] Marxism becomes the key site of Lyotard's rejection of the universal and commitment to the local and the particular. His blunt message is that it has not worked as a theory of social or political development and that it is time to come up with something to replace it that will not just make the same mistakes.

There is a sense of sadness about Lyotard's account of his break with Souyri, whom he clearly admired when they were colleagues in Pouvoir Ouvrier, but his antipathy to the grand narrative mentality means that reconciliation was never a realistic option. Marxists can only speak to Marxists and that to Lyotard sets up an unbreachable differend. To a sceptic the political world is, unfortunately enough, just full of these.

Other members of Socialisme ou Barbarie also moved away from Marxism and its contradictions, Cornelius Castoriadis being a promi-nent example. In his book *The Imaginary Institution of Society*, pub-lished just after *Libidinal Economy*, Castoriadis argued that Marxism had ossified as a revolutionary theory:

> [F]or over 40 years Marxism has become an *ideology* in the very sense that Marx gave to this term: a set of ideas that relate to a reality not in order to shed light on it and change it, but in order to veil it and to justify it in the imaginary, which permits people to say one thing and do another, to appear as other than they are.[53]

Castoriadis's unapologetic conclusion is that as a result of this pro-cess, 'Marxism is dead as a theory', a sentiment with which the Lyotard of *Libidinal Economy* and onwards could not but agree.[54] For neither of them is reform of Marxism from within a possibility; its contradictions just will not allow that to happen. That being the case, the only alternative is to turn away from it – as so many others on the left were to do in the closing decades of the twentieth century.

The Answer to Grand Narrative: The Postmodern Condition

Marxism was the epitome of a grand narrative for Lyotard, as he made crystal clear in *The Postmodern Condition*, dismissing the entire notion of a dialectic of history which could be controlled and directed by a revolutionary movement. He argued that we should react with 'incredulity' towards such an idea, which failed to capture the sheer variety of human experience and complexity of social development.[55] Grand narratives inhibited human creativity, which could be seen at its best in the phenomenon of the little narrative, particularly in the area of science. 'Postmodern science', as Lyotard perceived it (more than somewhat controversially to many in the scientific profession, however), was an inherently subversive practice, generating paradoxes instead of reinforcement of universal theories. The Grand Unified Theory that physicists were ostensibly searching for always appeared to be somewhere over the horizon (as it still is), with new findings frequently throwing the enquiry off course. On those grounds postmodern science constituted for Lyotard a model for how to challenge authoritarian systems in general; in each case they were founded on an illusion, the illusion that total control was possible. There was no such thing as a final answer to any line of human thought or political practice: merely new sets of phrases which others could link on to and go on doing so indefinitely, with no question of anyone being able to master the process in its entirety. The explicit message to ideologues and dogmatists is that nothing can be fixed in stone – except by the self-defeating use of force, a tactic which merely reveals the gaps in their belief system, especially when it is being deployed, as it so often is, to suppress a differend. Science, to Lyotard, was an area where differends just had to be accepted, being a natural consequence of scientific research exploring the boundaries of its subject – as it is duty-bound to be – and generating anomalies that put existing theories into question. Science will always be a work in progress.

Lyotard's dismissal of the claims of recent grand narratives has not, however, been borne out all that well by political developments since then. Fascism, Islamic fundamentalism and the general rise of the far right throughout the Western democracies all pose awkward questions about Lyotard's analysis in that respect, suggesting that he significantly underestimated the pull of the grand narrative idea, its sheer resilience and ability to keep reasserting itself. The fact that much of the far right sentiment in Europe has been directed against the European Union is an intriguing aspect of contemporary politics. It is possible to see Brexit as a challenge to grand narrative, with the EU cast in the role of a would-be super-state growing ever more ambitious and imperialist in its aims. It is an argument that has been put forward regularly by the Brexit side, who see the EU as an increasingly bureaucratic organisation bent on eroding the UK's sovereignty, and many have been convinced by it. Far from being a case of little narrative versus grand narrative, however, behind the Brexit campaign lies a residual grand narrative based on the power and might of the vanished British empire: grand narrative as nostalgia, as it were (or perhaps the UK's very own hauntology). There is a distinct differend on view here, where the present can only be talked about with Brexiteers in terms of a past that not even all of the population of the UK believes in any longer. The EU cannot be debated with on these terms, which involve incompatible language games, as if two imperialist worldviews were clashing with each other, unable to find any common ground for dialogue: dissension without any prospect of invention, just breakdown of communications. Some incredulity would not go amiss here, particularly as regards the supposed glory days of the British empire, which to the massed ranks of its colonised people was a differend on the grand scale that kept them largely subservient – and certainly eroded their sovereignty. Grand narratives can have a depressingly long half-life in that respect, to the extent of making an 'evil book' of one's own seem a very tempting prospect.[56] Debating with dogmatists is exhausting and rarely a successful activity: at some point an outburst of anger in the manner of *Libidinal Economy* can feel like the most therapeutic thing to do. Brexit and the Trump presidency can certainly cause such a reaction in many of us in the field of theory, confronted as we are by the most closed of closed minds, who are adamant that their beliefs alone are true.

Therapeutic as such an expression of rage might be, it is not a very defensible position academically, I admit. But rational argument eventually hits a wall in such cases and it is both frustrating and depressing to keep having to fight battles that you thought were won long ago: battles for equal rights regardless of race, colour, creed or gender, for example. Or with having to come up with arguments to answer the sheer stupidity of antisemitism or white supremacism. It can sometimes feel as if the Enlightenment never really happened, and tolerance of and respect for other beliefs and lifestyles has been steadily vanishing from the public sphere as dogmatism has asserted itself ever more insidiously there – to the extent that we might even start thinking of this as the 'Age of Dogmatism'. Reconciling oneself to the fact that bigotry can keep emerging, even in the most politically advanced of countries in the West, can be emotionally very wearing. A sense of despair on the part of the critical theorist or philosopher is not so hard to understand under those circumstances. Differends such as the above ought by now to be mere historical memories, like reading about the persecution of witches or the burning of heretics, or any actions or beliefs that we have long since recognised the irrationality of and therefore have banished from public discourse.

It is possible to wonder if Lyotard goes too far in his rejection of grand narratives, however, in that he only seems to see their bad side and considers that this always has to prevail. Grand narratives, in other words, can be defended – up to a point, anyway. They can have some very positive features, giving individuals a sense of belonging and a purpose to their lives. It depends what the grand narrative in question stands for, of course, but Enlightenment rationalism and fascism hardly seem moral equivalents, being very far apart in their objectives (and the same reservation applies as regards Enlightenment rationalism and any of the major monotheisms). Lyotard tends to lump all grand narratives together as if there was no meaningful difference between them, all of them only interested in gaining power and holding on to it, ruthlessly if need be. This is true in many instances, where dogmatism remains a real problem, yet it seems harsh when it comes to such a well-intentioned cultural movement as Enlightenment rationalism, which most commentators would say has left the world a generally better place, even if some interpretations of it (Marxism, as a case in point) have been used to justify repression. Neither is liberal democracy, even in its present imperfect form, quite the same thing as theocracy. While Lyotard is quite right to draw our attention to all the desperate actions that grand narrative has been used to justify, and is persuasive in his arguments against their power and influence and how these can so often be abused, that need not mean that no grand narrative can ever be trusted or that its positive side could not be resurrected and made to work for the public good. Communism did immense harm over the course of the twentieth century, but in the first instance it offered an Enlightenment-derived vision of a more egalitarian and less economically exploitative society that genuinely exerted wide popular appeal – and drew many Western intellectuals into its orbit as supporters. Lyotard is certainly not recommending a return to a pre-Enlightenment culture or state of mind, but his blanket rejection of the grand narrative phenomenon tends to close off debate on this issue, and does seem to signal something of a lapse into prejudgement on his part; he is not prepared to give any example of it the benefit of the doubt, or the intellectuals offering their support either. Even so, it is Marxism's tragedy that communism turned out the way it did, squandering the considerable store of goodwill it had initially generated by its trenchant critique of *laissez-faire* capitalism and mass industrialisation and its plans to overcome these and build a fairer society. Lyotard is one of the key players in the reaction to that, putting the case for a society where politics and belief are less rigid and more in the open-ended spirit of paganism. But he does underestimate the psychological pull of the grand narrative principle; it is not as simple to overcome that as he would appear to think. Grand narrative has plainly not faded away and shows little sign of doing so at present.

The Viability of Post-Marxism

Whether post-Marxism is a viable position to adopt in the contemporary political situation does need to be considered. Marxism itself no longer has much of a presence in left-wing political circles in the West and is very much a fringe activity there, confronted by an ever more confident far right increasing its influence within official governmental circles and actively seeking political power. Neither is post-Marxism, as we have seen, a homogeneous movement: it covers a wide range of responses from the desire to reform Marxist doctrine found in the work of Laclau and Mouffe, to the outright rejection of it as a system of thought by both Lyotard and Baudrillard. Much in the manner of scepticism, post-Marxism is a negative type of theory, telling you what its followers are against rather than what they are actually for collectively and that has to reduce its overall political impact; grand narrative is skilled at finding ways of filling the gap that ensues in such cases. Post-Marxists dislike Marxism's disposition towards authoritarianism and totalitarianism, but where they want to go from there and how much of Marx to take with them on the way is not always very clear. Nevertheless, Derrida is probably right to say that Marx's legacy cannot be avoided and that everyone on the left has to take that into account in the formulation of their political position, even if that does leave it very open as to what role Marx's thought has to play in current ideological struggles. Multiple Marxes are one thing, but their most likely effect is to fragment the left even further than it now finds itself (the great fear of classical Marxism, hence its obsession with maintaining strict obedience to the party line). What post-Marxism ought to lead to is a healthy respect for dissent within the left movement, not to continual infighting in which political credibility is frittered away – precisely what the far right would want to happen to make its takeover bid of the political realm all the easier to prosecute.

Lyotard becomes a very symbolic figure in this questioning of Marxism from within and then in the consequent breakaway from its grand narrative by so many of those critics, demonstrating both the strengths and the weaknesses of moving out of the Marxist framework. Being a grand narrative was always a plus point for Marxism, in that it appeared to offer a whole new lifestyle based on a system which was designed to replace the capitalist model – a model which had led to massive disparities in wealth wherever it was applied and which continues to do so under a neoliberal economic regime where the *laissez-faire* principle is being pushed to its limits, as the growing ranks of the precariat can testify. The solidarity that Marxism entailed could be very attractive to individuals aware of their personal vulnerability in the face of capitalist hegemony (something Lyotard is very concerned about too). Being part of a larger movement with a clear plan of action could be very empowering, and communism exerted just such an appeal well into the twentieth century; it has to be said that Lyotard's analysis of grand narrative is light on the psychological side. Without a grand narrative, however, it becomes considerably more difficult to stand up to the forces of capitalism, and anyone who has ever been influenced by Marxist thought will recognise the gap that opens up when that influence begins to wane: ready-made answers to political problems are no longer available and it is not always obvious what the most effective course of action would be to take. When that happens, left-wing thinkers find themselves being pushed back onto more nebulous methods of opposition, such as the activist efforts of emerging social movements for Laclau and Mouffe and, in Lyotard's case, little narratives with their limited, often very localised, objectives. The effectiveness of such small-scale activism has to be open to question, however, in that it does not necessarily point to a unified plan to challenge the dominant system seriously; in other words, it offers less sense of solidarity than a mass movement does, and that has to be seen as a definite weakness in a climate where fascist views are beginning to create their own version of that phenomenon. The disadvantages of a localised imperative have to be pointed out as well, although that is not to be seen as an argument for lapsing into fatalism or nihilism; every little narrative has to start from somewhere, and the downside of reverting to the grand narrative style of politics is only too evident. It is a tension that is present throughout Lyotard's work, and one that all ex- and post-Marxists will experience. Lyotard's solution is to keep moving from little narrative to little narrative as circumstances alter, which demands a high level of ongoing critique that not all supporters of the left would probably be able to maintain, especially given his radically non-doctrinaire approach to tactics. One suspects that little narrative fatigue would soon set in for many and grand narrative could only gain from that, offering a sense of continuity that, it has to be conceded, does have its attractions – the psychological aspect coming into play again.

Leon Trotsky claimed that the Communist Party in the Soviet Union had 'betrayed' the revolution it had led, degenerating into an oppressive bureaucracy rather than delivering the expected dictatorship of the proletariat, and the theme of betrayal is one that regularly crops up in post-Marxist thought, of classical Marxism having failed to live up to its promises and thus losing its credibility.[57] Adorno and Horkheimer argued that our Enlightenment legacy had been betrayed, both by capitalist and communist society; Lyotard, that the FLN was on course to betray the Algerian masses in the aftermath of the successful anti-colonialist revolution there and that the French Communist Party (PCF) betrayed the left in the 1968 *événements* in Paris; Baudrillard, that excessive commitment to production in Marxist social practice had betrayed humanity's hopes of greater liberation by subordinating us to that relentless, soul-destroying process; Laclau and Mouffe, that the path to radical democracy had been betrayed by constant recourse to the theory of bourgeois hegemony to hide Marxism's theoretical weaknesses. All such critiques tell us how to fight Marxist orthodoxy more than they do how to take on the neoliberal capitalist machine (a global force with all the power and influence that implies) or the increasingly popular fascist right. Whether Lyotard is an idealist or a nihilist in his pursuit of dissension does need to addressed, because it could be seen as a very isolating activity on the part of the individual. Whether a permanent state of dissension is a feasible way to live, either individually or collectively, is also very much open to question, and it is an issue that I will keep coming back to over the rest of this study (as I will Lyotard's nihilistic streak, which some commentators have interpreted as a positive aspect of his thought). What also needs to be reiterated, however, is that Lyotard feels the current state of politics demands such a response if grand narratives are to be prevented from increasing their power. Dissension is a commitment not to give up that struggle, although its effects have to keep being assessed as situations change: philosophical politics makes very considerable demands of its followers, whether it is the state or capital that is the object of their attention at any given moment.

Conclusion

Lyotard's contribution to the post-Marxist moment brings to light both its advantages and disadvantages as a theoretical turn on the left. His Algerian writings suggest that he was possibly never more than a somewhat half-hearted Marxist in the first place, well aware of the problems that its theoretical inflexibility posed for an under-developed nation – and, by implication, more widely than that. It is the political rather than the philosophical impact of Marxism that Lyotard always concentrates on. As a theorist he wants to get down to the particular, and that is where a universalising theory such as Marxism, with its commitment to the command economy principle, is most vulnerable to criticism, seeing the big picture at the expense of the small. Lyotard favours local solutions, and that goes against the grain of the totalising imperative, with its explicitly authoritarian manner of proceeding, designed to facilitate the implementation of its all-encompassing theory. That concern with the particular and the local over the general and the totalising will become ever more pronounced over the course of Lyotard's career, as he develops concepts such as little narrative and paganism as the basis for his philosophical politics. It is an approach which could only put him on a collision course with Marxism, with the invective-laden text of *Libidinal Economy* the logical conclusion (and a valuable one in bringing leftist discontent out into the open, I would argue, despite his own reservations about its somewhat hysterical tone). Laclau and Mouffe's championship of new social movements also put them on a collision course with the Marxist establishment, providing yet another example of the particular and the local being preferred to an authoritarian grand narrative. Lyotard was in the vanguard of that attack on Marxism's top-down ethos, but his switch to tactics as a means of challenging grand narrative does bring out the weakness of the post-Marxist position. Compared to Marxism itself it can all look a bit improvised and far harder to organise opposition around. Organising opposition was one of the strongest points of communism, the highest-profile movement within Marxism, its objectives and programme for achieving these always being perfectly clear; post-Marxism constitutes a much vaguer prospect when it comes to campaigning.

What Lyotard's development as a thinker signals is the individualistic quality of post-Marxism, which is intellectually more honest, perhaps, certainly in its opposition to authoritarianism and totalitarianism, but politically less effective when it comes to constructing mass protest against your ideological enemy. Philosophical politics will always appear a niche position in such respects. It is a tension that Lyotard has to keep negotiating in his work, but, as suggested above, I do think it is intellectually more honest than pretending that grand narrative holds the answers to all our problems – a temptation that all too many find hard to resist. Post-Marxists have to re-create their politics from scratch, with a lack of guidelines as to how to do this: the 'post-' leaves a large gap that can be very difficult to fill, and that can give rise to sensations of haunting. Lyotard is a case study in how to work one's way out of that quandary, as well as of the residual problems that will keep cropping up on the journey.

Notes

1. Marx and Engels, *The Communist Manifesto*, p. 86.
2. Lyotard, *Just Gaming*, p. 25.
3. Laclau and Mouffe, 'Post-Marxism Without Apologies', p. 106.
4. Lyotard, *Libidinal Economy*, p. 115.
5. Ibid., pp. 95–6.
6. Ibid., p. 107.
7. Ibid., p. 96.
8. Sartre, *What is Literature?*, p. 190.
9. Ibid., p. 189.
10. Lyotard, *The Postmodern Condition*, p. xxv.
11. Anderson, *Considerations on Western Marxism*, p. 25.
12. Lukács, *History and Class Consciousness*, p. 1.
13. Adorno and Horkenheimer, *Dialectic of Enlightenment*, p. xiii.
14. Ibid., p. xv.
15. Adorno, *Negative Dialectics*, p. 136.
16. Lyotard, *Peregrinations*, p. 12.
17. Lyotard, *The Postmodern Condition*, p. xxv.
18. Hindess and Hirst, *Pre-Capitalist Modes of Production*, p. 308.
19. Standing, *The Precariat*.
20. See, for example, Gorz, *Farewell to the Working Class*.
21. Baudrillard, *The Mirror of Production*, pp. 59–60.
22. Lyotard, *Libidinal Economy*, p. 96.
23. Althusser and Balibar, *Reading Capital*, p. 13.
24. Lyotard, *Libidinal Economy*, p. 96.
25. Adorno, *Negative Dialectics*, p. 47.
26. See Gramsci, *Selections from the Prison Notebooks*.

27. '[I]t is ultimately the ruling ideology which is realized in the Ideological State Apparatuses', Althusser, *Lenin and Philosophy and Other Essays*, p. 146.
28. Adorno and Horkheimer, *Dialectic of Enlightenment*, p. xiv.
29. Derrida, *Specters of* Marx, pp. 13, 14.
30. Ibid., p. 10.
31. Lyotard, *Peregrinations*, p. 63.
32. Derrida, *Specters of Marx*, p. 13.
33. See Carver, *The Postmodern Marx*, for a positive spin on the benefits of subjecting Marx's work to analysis through 'a mild form of postmodernism' (p. 2). Even 'mild', however, would be more than Marxist true believers would be prepared to countenance.
34. Gordon, *Ghostly Matters*, pp. 7, xvi.
35. Lyotard, 'Algeria Evacuated', in *Political Writings*, pp. 293–326 (p. 302).
36. Ibid., p. 302.
37. Lyotard, *Peregrinations*, p. 27.
38. Lyotard, 'Algerian Contradictions Exposed', in *Political Writings*, pp. 197–213 (p. 198).
39. Lyotard, *Peregrinations*, p. 27.
40. Ibid., p. 13.
41. Lyotard, *Libidinal Economy*, p. 96.
42. Lyotard, *Driftworks*, p. 91.
43. Lyotard, *Peregrinations*, p. 13.
44. Lyotard, *Libidinal Economy*, p. 96.
45. Ibid., p. 95.
46. Lyotard, *The Differend*, p. 171.
47. Ibid., p. 171.
48. Lyotard, 'A Memorial of Marxism: For Pierre Souyri', in *Peregrinations*, pp. 45–75 (p. 49).
49. Ibid., p. 51.
50. Ibid., p. 49.
51. Ibid., p. 61.
52. Ibid., p. 53.
53. Castoriadis, *The Imaginary Institution of Society*, p. 11.
54. Ibid., p. 63.
55. Lyotard, *The Postmodern Condition*, p. xxiv.
56. Apologists can still be found for the British empire, however; see, for example, Ferguson, *Empire*.
57. See Trotsky, *The Revolution Betrayed*.

Chapter 4

The Politics of the Differend

The differend is arguably the most resonant of Lyotard's concepts, in that it describes a situation that has arisen repeatedly throughout world history and continues to bedevil political life in our own day. Outlined in the work of that name, a differend is an ostensibly irreconcilable dispute and dealing with it constitutes for Lyotard one of the most critical tests of a political system – a test that few deal with all that well.[1] In ideological terms of reference the parties on each side of the dispute – colonists and the colonised, for example, or bosses and employees – are operating with a different set of rules, and neither side regards the other's set as legitimate, creating a situation where misunderstandings proliferate to problematise relationships, often to the point of breakdown (a recurrent event in colonies particularly). There is no common ground between them where meaningful debate could be conducted and accommodations reached. Historically, differends have most often been dealt with by recourse to violence or repression and that creates long-term resentments that can eventually undermine a society's stability quite severely. Racial and ethnic clashes within countries are particularly pertinent examples of how that can happen, and they are rife in the contemporary world, where multiculturalism is more of an ideal to which lip service is paid by governments and institutions than a successfully implemented policy (yet more evidence of bigotry's dogged persistence). Race in particular is one of the most intractable differends of our time, as American life alone provides ample evidence for, with relations between black and white Americans always somewhat strained and sometimes openly hostile – the Trump presidency's white supremacist bias has not helped matters in that respect. Lyotard conceived of ideological difference as being like an archipelago, where each island had its own rules and procedures which applied only within that specific territory. The significance of that notion in geopolitical terms, as a corrective to the bullying tactics so often deployed by the major world powers (with the USA under the Trump presidency a serial offender), will be analysed to consider what impact it could have on international relations. As with a little narrative based parliamentary system, a thought experiment would seem a useful way of exploring the likely advantages and disadvantages of Lyotard's major concepts.

The Archipelago and Differends

The archipelago is Lyotard's metaphor for the way language games work, or should work anyway, each island being a self-contained entity expecting allegiance to its rules when within its territories, but acknowledging the validity of the rules applied on other islands and not seeking to interfere in any of these. Difference is the accepted state of affairs, respected by all parties. The concept represents something of an ideal world for Lyotard, picturing a situation where each island is left free to express its own language game and follow its own chosen lifestyle, without having to worry about what its neighbours are doing. If international politics worked that way then there would be little friction between nations, but as we know from long experience this is just not the case; in geopolitical terms differends are constantly being created by clashes between competing grand narratives, which are just as much a feature of our own age as they ever have been. Nation states repeatedly fail the test of the differend, and geopolitics is one long series of dealings with the fall-out from these – very often desperate effects such as war or ethnic cleansing. Lyotard wants to keep all language games discrete in the style of the archipelago, however, in order to maintain their integrity and lower the incidence of differends; the language game of justice must not be infiltrated by others, particularly that of a grand narrative, for example, or its decisions will be compromised.

Lyotard devises the notion of the archipelago to explain the relationship he sees between Kant's various critiques, where the so-called 'third' critique, the *Critique of Judgment*, was designed to bridge the gap Kant himself identified as existing between the *Critique of Pure Reason* and the *Critique of Practical Reason*. In Lyotard's reading, however, the gap was not bridged, with each work involving different sets of criteria and objectives that meant they ought to be kept separate. Although there are passages between them, these do not allow the criteria of one to be transferred to any of the others. The autonomy of each critique is insisted upon by Lyotard: the world of the sublime is not the world of pure or practical reason and they cannot be reconciled. I will return to this issue in the last chapter, but the key point to note here is that Lyotard rejects Kant's claim to

70

have devised a unified philosophical system. As ever, Lyotard is on the lookout for the incommensurabilities that most philosophers are concerned to overcome – and incommensurabilities signal differends, which takes us into a whole new philosophical and political situation.

It can sound all very tidy to keep philosophical projects apart in this way as if they were playing different language games, but, as Lyotard is only too well aware, in the real world language games are forever intruding on each other and grand narratives are constantly trying to manipulate them to their own ends, being convinced of their own innate superiority. Keeping the language game of politics, invariably the preserve of grand narrative, out of the language game of justice is an ideal that runs directly counter to current ideological practice, where the justice system is seen to be an integral part of the political system by the ruling authorities. The judiciary are meant to be independent, but there are various ways around this that politicians can fall back on if they want to exert influence. In many countries judiciary appointments are under the direct control of the central government (as the Supreme Court is in the USA, for example), which opens up the prospect of a certain degree of manipulation by the political authorities. Appointments to the Supreme Court of the United States will generally reflect the ideological bias of the President in office (as has happened with Donald Trump) and for all the complaints this can cause from the other party, the system permits it and will no doubt continue to do so as new Presidents take up office. It is now a well-established precedent. In totalitarian states there is not even the pretence of an independent judiciary, as was the case in the Soviet Union where the Communist Party controlled all aspects of public life and the judiciary was there to do its bidding (as in the notorious 'show trials' of the Stalinist era, when even the semblance of legal due process was dispensed with).

In a sense, every democracy runs the risk of generating a differend when there is a general election. Whichever party wins a majority has to rule over the disappointed minority too, and there is always a chance that if its ideological programme is considered too radical, then it may well alienate much of the minority in putting it into practice. Most of the time this is accepted by the minority, with either good or bad grace, but it can be a tricky situation to negotiate if the governing majority is either very far left or very far right in character, thus out of the minority's ideological comfort zone (where Mouffe's 'shared adhesion' to liberal democratic values applies, for example). The Brexit referendum also posed an awkward test for the UK's governmental model, in that the Leave and Remain sides were so bitterly divided by the result that there was not enough of a public consensus to agree to any of the options on offer, leading to accusations of treason and betrayal being freely traded in both parliament and the media; the stalemate that resulted was always claimed to be the other side's fault. The Leave side held the upper hand with their 52 per cent majority, but despite the apparent democratic vindication that gave, the gulf between the two sides was so wide that it really did seem as if they were using different language games, thus rendering their positions incompatible. Democracy's weak points came vividly into view in this instance, especially when the possibility of compromise was repeatedly ruled out. Trump's presidency created a similarly critical situation on the American political scene, with pro- and anti-Trump factions both disputing the legitimacy of the other's beliefs and principles, and constant accusations of fake news serving to separate them even further from each other. The clash between post-truth and truth that Trump's presidency cultivated so cynically constituted an almost classic example of a differend, although it is more problematic to think that bearing witness was the proper attitude to adopt towards this. Deception surely deserves a stronger response: fake news invalidates the whole political process, making it all but impossible to know whom you can trust, thus dealing a further blow to our supposed Enlightenment heritage of rational debate.[2] Democracy yet again seemed badly caught out by developments that did not fit its model, and the fake news/alternative facts scandal is a story which has not yet run its course, a prime example of the 'rebellious politics' that liberal democrats, no less than Lyotard, are struggling to master.

Gender and the Differend

The issue of whether gender qualifies as a differend is worth some consideration, opening the debate out as it does into gender and sexual politics. Lyotard does raise this prospect in 'She's' monologue in 'Can Thought Go On Without a Body' in *The Inhuman*, without coming to any definite conclusion; as She observes: 'I don't know whether sexual difference is ontological difference. How would a person *know*?'.[3] There is no doubt that some schools of feminist thought treat it as such, especially those that encourage separatism, and they could certainly come up with a precise answer to She's question, most likely pointing out that patriarchy has traditionally assumed an equivalence between the sexual and the ontological, with women being the ones to suffer the adverse social and political consequences. Women were to be treated as weak and emotional beings while men were strong and rational – and thus the ones who had to be in charge. The work of Luce Irigaray and Hélène Cixous can be mentioned in this context, for example: as far as they are concerned, biology effectively creates a differend between the male and female sex (a 'gendifferend', as it were). It is a differend that works very much to the benefit of men, with an entrenched social tradition of patriarchy that has involved various forms of oppression for women globally for most of human history, power being an overwhelmingly male preserve, the 'glass ceiling' maintaining this very effectively. Feminism has been an attempt to challenge that system, and it has met with a certain amount of success in that regard in the West, although far less so in the non-Western world where patriarchal cultures still largely hold sway, often reinforced by the dominant religion (monotheistic religions traditionally being strongly patriarchal in bias). Equal opportunities has become more and more of an issue in Western society, with concerted campaigns to reduce inequalities in the workplace and in public life in general. The goal is to abolish discrimination on gender grounds, although it still exists in hidden forms in many areas: equal pay is still a point of considerable contention, for example, if one that is gradually being addressed. Women are still under-represented in many areas of public life as well, as in the case of politics, which, despite a few high-profile figures, basically remains a male domain governed by male codes of behaviour that women can find very alienating if they do ever manage to break through the glass ceiling into the system's governing bodies.

Irigaray emphasises difference to the point when it effectively becomes a differend separating the sexes, insisting that '[s]exual difference is one of the major philosophical issues, if not the issue, of our age' and that '[a] revolution in thought and ethics is needed if the work of sexual difference is to take place'.[4] Separate development would be one way of achieving this, and Irigaray's work implies that, although it has to be said that it has met with opposition from within the feminist community as well as, far more predictably, from within patriarchal circles determined to preserve their privileges. Irigaray's argument is that patriarchy has meant that women have been turned into 'a more or less obliging prop for the enactment of man's fantasies', with female emotional and sexual needs being largely ignored.[5] Reforming patriarchy from within seems like a pointless exercise to thinkers like Irigaray; men's and

73

women's nature and experience just do not overlap enough to make this feasible, as she points out in an interview:

> [W]oman engenders *in herself*, makes love *in herself*. Man engenders and makes love *outside of himself*. This means that their relationship to themselves and their relationship to the other are far from being similar, favoring either the inside *or* the outside, either refuge in oneself *or* respect for the other outside of oneself.[6]

This certainly sounds like a prototypical differend, and Irigaray is quite explicit about the gulf that separates the sides: 'From birth, men and women belong to different worlds, biologically and relationally' (contrary to Simone de Beauvoir's claim, for Irigaray one *is* born a woman).[7] We are dealing, as her book's subtitle puts it, with 'a culture of two subjects', two subjects who can develop only in their own unique, differential way.

Cixous's concept of *écriture féminine* makes a similar assumption about a differend-style difference between the sexes that demands radical action be taken to correct the current imbalance: 'Woman must write her self: must write about women and bring women to writing, from which they have been driven away as violently as from their bodies ... I write woman: woman must write woman. And man, man'.[8] To bear witness from this perspective is to withdraw from the patriarchal system and develop female culture without male intervention. Separatist gender politics certainly seems to support the notion of the differend and to regard it as the basis for a sustained challenge on patriarchy, which historically has worked to suppress that differend in order to maintain its own power structure, something that the institutional structures of most cultures makes very apparent from religion through politics. Opting out altogether seems a logical enough response to such a history of entrenched male cultural dominance, to thinkers like Iragaray and Cixous the only way that women can take control of their own destiny.

Separatism is an extreme position which, as mentioned above, has not been accepted by all feminists as the best tactic to bring about change in patriarchy; activism from within is still the most common approach adopted and it has generated a series of little narratives which have been meeting with a certain amount of success. In practical terms it is hard to see how separatism could be made to work on a large scale, assuming as it does a society constructed on the lines of apartheid, which is rarely a popular idea; but Lyotard's concept of the archipelago does have some affinities with it that are worth considering all the same. The self-contained units of the Lyotardean archipelago each have their own line of development and internal regulations. Each island is expected to respect the systems of all the others without interfering in their operation, so it is possible to imagine gender difference being drawn up along similar lines, where there would be a variety of positions on offer, with their own institutional networks in support (even to the extent of legal and political ones). Moving from one to the other position would be to agree to follow the new set of rules as to behaviour and beliefs found there, rather in the manner of paganism where each city has its own pantheon of gods. Critically, there would be no attempt made to overthrow any particular belief system by imposing that of another island on the inhabitants: the colonial mentality is to have no place in such a context. The LGBT community in general would be supportive of such a system, which would leave them free to follow their particular sexual orientation without fear of discrimination. It is admittedly an idealistic scenario and would need a lot of thinking through as to how to organise it, but it is not an impossible one.

As indicated above, Lyotard is to raise the issue of gender difference in *The Inhuman*, when discussing the characteristics that computers should have if they were to replace humanity after the death of the sun. There is a case to be made that computers should be programmed to include gender traits, as She suggests, although how that could be done is not really explored (never mind the willingness of the corporate sector to pursue such a goal that would seem unnecessary to them in terms of operational efficiency). Nor is whether this would make the notion of gender actually outlive humanity in any but the most abstract of ways (whether it could have any meaning at all to the machines is very open to question). It is an intriguing idea, however, that will be dealt with in more detail in the analysis of Lyotard's concept of the inhuman in Chapter 6.

The Nation State and the Differend

International politics raises some interesting issues with regard to the differend. At least in theory nation states act as if they were in an archipelago, with the concept of national sovereignty giving them control of their own territory and political system and differentiating them from their neighbours. National sovereignty is taken to guarantee each nation's separate identity and its right to defend itself from any encroachments made on that. That is a principle which international bodies like the United Nations operate by, but in practice it is never quite that straightforward. For a start, nations have to trade with each other if they are to develop their economy and this usually will involve accepting certain restrictions or agreeing to alter some of their social or political practices. There are few nations around the world that are not tied into such deals, which generally mean adhering to standards set by various international bodies (on tariffs, etc.). When it comes to institutions like the European Union, this can become very complex in that it requires its members to follow a common set of rules which often appear to override national sovereignty. Only the EU, for example, can negotiate new trade deals with outside partners, not the individual member countries themselves, and all member countries have to comply with any rulings made by the European Parliament in Brussels on the workings of the common market and customs union. At least in part, Brexit was a reaction to this state of affairs and the Leave campaign played this up as much as they could with the notorious slogan of 'taking back control'. What Brexit succeeded in demonstrating more than anything, however, was how difficult it is for any nation to stand completely alone in the current world order, where so many aspects of everyday life are so interconnected. Add to that the fact that the international financial markets make a mockery of the notion of taking back control anyway, when they can cause economies to collapse if they lose faith in their stability and reliability, withdrawing investment and causing their national currency to fall sharply in value. No nation state is proof against that, the markets being an amorphous entity spread around amongst all members of the international community, and it works against the more extreme conceptions of national sovereignty (with certain exceptions such as North Korea, which hardly constitutes much of a role model). There is a differend between theory and practice when it comes to the concept of sovereignty, particularly when it applies to small to middle-size nations (the UK being in that group), and that is not always recognised by their political class. Or perhaps one should say not acknowledged, because to do so would be to admit to the limitations of their particular grand narrative and therefore risk losing their credibility – and the power that follows on from that. Delusions of grandeur are all too common when it comes to the political class.

The archipelago principle does assume a fairly discrete form of national sovereignty, which it would be very difficult to maintain as international relations are currently constructed (trade wars can easily become real wars, for example, and history is full of such cases), although Lyotard does not really develop the notion very far in hard political terms. That tendency to separate out phenomena to prevent the emergence of differends is a characteristic of Lyotard's thought, and while it may be considered overly idealistic, and by his critics as just too convenient an argument, it nevertheless suggests some ways of reducing the incidence of differends in the political arena. Although it is in favour of discrete sovereignties, it is opposed to dogmatic ones (Brexit providing a classic example of how the two could be confused), and dogmatism provides a ready supply of differends, being dismissive of the idea of ever needing to bear witness. An archipelago based on dogmatism is not what Lyotard envisages as the point of the exercise; rather it is one that operates on pagan principles, where there is a much more free and easy attitude towards belief systems – and power too, come to that. Flexibility is the hallmark of the pagan system.

We can speculate how the archipelago system could be paganised to bring about such flexibility in the contemporary world, although it would require a significant shift of perspective as to how to conduct politics. Lyotard bases paganism on the model of Greek city states in the classical era, which implies a fairly localised form of political organisation; the Greek examples did have cultural connections, such as language, etc., but they remained discrete politically. In order to achieve such a system now, it would be necessary to have a far looser form of national sovereignty in operation than is the current norm, with a considerable amount of devolution at both regional and urban levels (city states taking in some of the surrounding rural area as part of their remit, as they did in classical Greece to provide basic food supplies). It would be a federal set-up carried to greater lengths than any existing model, with power centred on the city states rather than a national government. There are other examples of the city state system to consider, such as those in Italy during the medieval and Renaissance periods, and other loosely aggregated small state systems too, as in Italy and Germany in their pre-unified modern formulations. It is not difficult to envisage such systems, although it is difficult to work out how they would be policed to prevent them from encroaching on their neighbours in any way – as was plainly the case with the Italian city states, which were often at war with each other, as were Greek city states such as Sparta and Athens. As I have argued before, there is an anarchistic quality to much of Lyotard's political thinking, in that to work as he would want it to there has to be a substantial amount of goodwill around, an ability, in the well-worn phrase, 'to live and let live' (a dictum that has largely been honoured in the breach historically and that the far right of our own day certainly has no respect at all for). A pagan style of socio-political organisation assumes that no one harbours evil designs on others, or would be allowed to by their peers (as William Godwin's anarchist theories suggests would work as a corrective),[9] and that everyone's particular group – city state or whatever – is respected as an autonomous entity. In an anarchist ideal world, there would be no fascists, or totalitarians of any type, and authoritarianism would be frowned upon as a thing of the past. Marxist utopia makes the same kind of assumption: that the good side of human nature would drive out the bad if the right kind of social conditions could be instituted and that everyone would, in effect, live happily ever after. Ensuring universal compliance to this is where the problem lies, however, as it is with any utopian-inclined scheme; with the best will in the world, societies can rarely achieve political unanimity for any great length of time, or manage to eradicate bigotry either. Lyotard is unlikely to be arguing for this kind of utopia and would want to include dissension in it – but a creative dissension that did not collapse into socially debilitating conflict.

The implication of Lyotard's paganism is that it would be better if political power was exercised in much smaller units than the overarching nation state of modern times. The more devolved that power is then the less chance there is of any unit having the ability to engage in empire building (although it would have to be conceded that examples like classical era Rome, initially a small city state, of course, could be cited to the contrary). If the units were run on the little narrative principle then the likelihood of such a development occurring would be minimised even further (excluding a Roman model from emerging, hopefully); they provide the basis for working towards a less centralised political system. It would be a case of the local taking precedence over the global – or even the national. Political parties in the West are in principle in favour of devolution, although in practice they are generally reluctant to surrender very much of the power that they wield at national level. That would be a stumbling block to moving towards Lyotard's ideal, but the fact that such ideas are so regularly expressed and meet with a fair amount of public approval means that they could be built upon. Similar ideas are floated not just by anarchist thinkers, but by Green political groupings also, the notion being that we have to get down to local level to ensure that everyone feels involved in achieving their environmental goals and would work collectively towards realising them, recognising that it really is in the common interest to do so. I suppose it could be objected that this sounds like an ideological grand narrative, but as it can only be properly effective if it is carried out as a series of little narratives at local level, it could be argued that it escapes such a description and could be incorporated into a pagan political set-up.

Thought experiments of this kind will always come up against the hard reality of current practice, where, for all Lyotard's claims that their day is over, grand narrative ideologies still hold sway and seem able to command enough allegiance, from both 'intellectuals' and the general public, to continue dominating the political realm as they have been doing throughout the modern era. Some may fall behind, as Marxism notably did (and many of the major monotheisms too, Islam being the current exception), but the pattern is that others then expand their influence to fill the gap that has opened up. What Lyotard wants us to realise, however, is that there is no inevitability about this, that it can, and by him always will, be challenged; communism did fall, so might any other grand narrative. Putting grand narratives on the defensive can be thought of as a necessary first step towards a paganisation of politics.

Internal Differends

As individuals we are not immune from the differend on a personal basis; there can be differends within our own thought and daily interactions with others, and it can be quite enlightening to survey how we handle them (and more often than not, mishandle them). There can often be discrepancies between what we believe we should do and what we actually do, quite marked discrepancies too, and similarly between what we think we should believe and what we actually do believe; all of us could benefit from analysing this aspect of our character much more than we do.[10] There might be archipelagos, in the negative sense, within our own mind, compartmentalised from each other and with different sets of rules applying, often contradictory ones. The refugee situation (or crisis, as many commentators are now describing it) in Europe in the last few years has brought such discrepancies into focus quite sharply, in that most people can sympathise with the refugees' plight – bigots always excepted. Many of them are, after all, escaping from battle zones, civil wars or failed or rogue states which cannot guarantee their personal security, or even provide them with the basic necessities of life, so that it is small wonder they want to seek out better conditions elsewhere. Yet even so, we can still be uneasy about our own country taking in a significant amount of refugees to settle there – a definite, and embarrassing, clash of beliefs. On humanitarian grounds we ought to be in favour of providing sanctuary for those fleeing from such dangerous living conditions and although most of us in the West realise this, we can still be capable of feeling uncomfortable about the effect this might have on our own lifestyle – putting a strain on our nation's welfare system, for example, or even requiring higher taxes to be introduced to cover the costs of resettling the refugees. It is a reaction which has been seen in every Western European country over the last few years. Few of us will campaign actively to take in refugees, tending instead just to ignore the situation most of the time – until some news report jolts our conscience once again (generally to do with an overloaded boat going down somewhere in the Mediterranean, with consequent loss of life), generating a sense of guilt about our humanitarian failings. All this despite the fact that the far right exploits the crisis to foster resentment against immigrants, playing the national identity card quite shamelessly, and that this policy is attracting significant support in a series of national elections across Europe.

Those failings also become apparent if we think of the larger issue of world poverty, of which the refugee crisis is only a small part. A wide range of charity organisations keep trying to bring our attention to this issue through media advertising and leaflets delivered regularly through the post. Feelings of guilt are generated by these as well and while some donations might be made by us in consequence, most of the time we bury this issue at the back of our mind; we glance at the leaflets, then most likely bin them and just go on as usual ('compassion fatigue' as this has been dubbed, which nevertheless hardly excuses the action). Poverty is rampant internationally but not impinging on our daily lives. We would agree that something should be done to alleviate the condition, but rarely do anything very much about it. Ignoring such problems, or pretending that they do not exist, hardly qualifies as bearing witness and this is an internal struggle that almost all of us have to go through on a regular basis. Differends are not just a matter of competing ideologies or powers, therefore; they are an ever-present factor in our everyday lives and we should be able to learn from this personal experience how we ought to be dealing with them in the wider political domain. Perhaps we should all be monitoring our personal ability to compartmentalise beliefs in the style of an archipelago, such that we can hold contradictory ones without recognising the paradox that entails.

Another very topical example of a critical discrepancy between thought and action is climate change (now 'crisis' too, for many commentators). What needs to be done is well known, with various scientific bodies, such as the Intergovernmental Panel on Climate Change (IPCC), outlining the steps that will have to be taken to bring down the rate of carbon emissions into the atmosphere and thus prevent further overheating of the planet: steps that are now well overdue. Climate sceptics also make their views known, decrying the scientific evidence, and they constitute a very vocal lobby, well funded by the fossil fuel industry with its vested interest in carrying on as usual. Various other natural causes have been suggested for the warming (with studies to back them up),[11] yet it is probably fair to say that there is now a general consensus that climate change is happening and that human beings are the major cause of it – hence the coining of the term 'the anthropocene'. Some action has been taken, but its effect on the overall situation can be described as at best cosmetic. Small initiatives notwithstanding, the problem is not just still with us, it is getting steadily worse and speeding up in the process, raising the alarming prospect of irreversible tipping points occurring. What was once thought to be a problem that future generations would have to face up to (a century or two ahead or so) is in reality here now and affecting our lives in many ways such as extremes in weather conditions – these too are becoming far more frequent, as scientists had warned would be an entirely predictable result of climate change. Record-breaking heatwaves, for example, are now common occurrences and can leave a substantial toll of deaths in their wake, as too can the increasing incidence of droughts and forest fires, all part of the same pattern (which also includes ever more devastating hurricanes). 'The worst in recorded history' is becoming a standard term in weather reports. Campaigners rail against the lack of meaningful action by governments internationally, yet most of us carry on as we have always done, as if it was someone's else's problem and not ours. Despite that, we are aware we really ought to be doing something, such as voting for parties committed to putting systems in place to curb carbon emissions – and on a drastic basis if need be. The differend between thought and action is still there within our minds, however, and we are in general failing to respond to it as positively and systematically as we should, compartmentalising the issue instead. The major political parties in the West do much the same, their manifesto promises rarely being realised.

Conclusion

The differend asks us to see politics in a very different light than we are used to, emphasising that, contrary to the claims of traditional party politics, there are not always solutions to disputes and that it is counter-productive to pretend that there are, or to fall into the trap of thinking that force alone can close down an irreconcilable dispute. Any such 'solution' of the latter kind can only ever be artificial, an ideologically motivated way of masking symptoms rather than dealing with causes – and causes will not go away, just fester under the surface to create difficulties at a later point (that is also the problem with internal differends, so there is no escaping this situation; it will catch you too eventually with its own version of the 'return of the repressed'). Bearing witness requires us to move away from the confrontational style of politics and to look for ways of protecting difference. Lyotard makes this point repeatedly over the course of his career, although it has to be said that he does not provide a detailed set of instructions as to how to go about it. That is usually how political theories come to be judged, so it is a reasonable criticism to make of Lyotard's work; there is a gap there and it has to be acknowledged, even by Lyotard supporters. What the gap does, however, is to put it back on us as readers to think the issue through without recourse to a grand narrative – the position that Lyotard finds himself in as a post-Marxist, hence his reluctance to offer a specific method that could take on an air of authority. He does, however, make us very aware of what is at stake with difference and the demands it makes on us to come up with tactics, 'working hypotheses' in Lyotard's scheme of things, to enable it to be expressed and experienced as a positive force in our culture rather than a source of conflict and division. Dealing with the differend ought to concentrate all our minds on the critical importance of that task.

Notes

1. Lyotard, *The Differend*.
2. For more on this topic, see Sim, *Post-Truth, Scepticism and Power*.
3. Lyotard, 'Can Thought Go On Without a Body?', in *The Inhuman*, pp. 8–23 (p. 21).
4. Irigaray, *An Ethics of Sexual Difference*, pp. 5, 6.
5. Irigaray, *This Sex Which Is Not One*, p. 25.
6. Irigaray and Lotringer, *Why Different?*, p. 96.

7. Ibid., p. 96. 'One is not born, but rather becomes, a woman' (de Beauvoir, *The Second Sex*, p. 295).
8. Cixous, 'The Laugh of the Medusa', in Marks and de Courtivron, *New French Feminisms*, pp. 245–64 (pp. 245, 247).
9. Godwin believed that a political system based on the 'observant eye, of public judgement' would be enough to ensure good behaviour in every citizen, such that we could look forward to 'the dissolution of political government', the goal of all anarchist theorists (Godwin, *Enquiry Concerning Political Justice*, p. 554).
10. The breakdown in relations between Lyra and her daemon in Philip Pullman's *The Secret Commonwealth* might be seen as an imaginative rendering of an internal differend.
11. A recent study published in the journal *Scientific Reports*, for example (Zharkova et al., 'Oscillations of the Baseline of Solar Magnetic Field and Solar Irradiance on a Millennial Timescale'), claiming that changes in solar cycles could explain global warming, has come in for some severe criticism from several quarters (including scientists in NASA). There have even been calls for the paper to be withdrawn on the grounds of what one critic has described as 'elementary' mistakes in its data (see Adam Vaughan, 'Controversial Climate Study Under Investigation', p. 14).

Chapter 5

The Politics of Heidegger

The 'Heidegger Affair' of the 1980s brought some highly contentious political issues to the fore in French intellectual life – the Holocaust and antisemitism as particular cases in point. The 'Affair' was sparked off by Victor Farías's book *Heidegger and Nazism*, a history of Martin Heidegger's dealings with the Nazi regime, and it generated considerable controversy amongst French intellectuals, given that Heidegger's phenomenology had exerted such a powerful influence on French philosophy from Jean-Paul Sartre and the existentialist movement onwards. Many French thinkers, notably Jacques Derrida, felt motivated to defend Heidegger on the grounds that his philosophy ought to be kept separate from his life, a not unreasonable position to adopt; but others, like Lyotard, took a much more critical stance. For Lyotard, Heidegger was guilty of the sin of 'forgetting' the Holocaust in the post-war years, refusing to apologise for his role in the Nazi movement, or even actively acknowledging it. (Although one might be cynical and wonder just how much difference an apology from such a figure would have made to those who survived the event or had lost family members in it; some things go beyond such gestures.) This was exactly what the concept of a philosophical politics was designed to counter: philosophers were expected to bear witness to the evils of their times, not to turn their back on them if that made their lives easier. Heidegger was an altogether more problematic case in that he could be accused of actual collusion with that evil. In *Heidegger and "the jews"* Lyotard argued that the historical treatment of the Jewish race was symptomatic of a deep-seated commitment to social homogeneity in Western culture that was intolerant of any minority that did not conform to its belief system and the values this entailed: a differend that was always in play and that kept needing to be drawn to our attention because of the extensive catalogue of abuses it generated. With antisemitism on the rise in recent years and anti-immigrant prejudices becoming increasingly evident in election campaigns throughout Europe, social homogeneity and multi-culturalism coming into open conflict with each other in consequence, Lyotard's arguments are assuming greater importance. Essentially, they are arguments against populism, which is turning into a dominating factor in contemporary politics, and this chapter will address how they can contribute to that debate, particularly the vexed issue of right versus left populism.[1]

Farías on Heidegger

Farías's book makes it hard to ignore Heidegger's ideological leanings, which he maps out in considerable detail over the course of the Nazi regime in Germany. There can be no doubt that Heidegger benefited from his Nazi connections, as in his appointment as Rector of Freiburg University shortly after the Nazis came to power in 1933. He was the sort of figure who was useful to the Nazis, providing intellectual weight to their socio-political programme. This was a role played by Richard Strauss in the musical world, Strauss being appointed the first president of the Reich Music Chamber, set up by the Ministry of Propaganda, and so becoming complicit with the regime's hostility towards Jewish composers (although he did demonstrate a surprising degree of naivete in continuing to work with Jewish collaborators, such as the librettist Hugo von Hofmannsthal, on his operas for quite some time afterwards). Given the flight of so many high-profile intellectual and artistic figures from Germany after the Nazi takeover, including Bertolt Brecht, Kurt Weill, Walter Benjamin and the Frankfurt School of Social Theory (T. W. Adorno, Max Horkheimer and Herbert Marcuse amongst others), Heidegger and Strauss can hardly evade some sort of judgement for cooperating with the new regime. Exactly what this means in terms of their professional work, however, remains much more difficult to determine, although there has never as such been any prohibition placed on it. The 'Affair' notwithstanding, Heidegger continues to be studied in philosophy departments around the world, and Strauss's music is regularly performed in concert halls and opera houses. Many who either study or listen to their work are probably largely unaware of their past, and might regard it as irrelevant now anyway.

Derrida on Heidegger

Derrida's approach to Heidegger's work in the aftermath of Farías's book actually has a great deal to commend it. Almost any cultural figure from the past carries ideological baggage that might be disapproved of nowadays (by at least some section of the population,

85

especially given the growth of identity politics), and it would be highly reductive to avoid their work on those grounds. Derrida's claim is that any such figure's ideas can be adapted by both the right and the left, meaning that the ideas are always open to interpretation (Lyotard's concept of thought as clouds would seem to allow for that outcome as well, since its premise is that thought as such belongs to no one individual):

> There can always be a Hegelianism of the left and a Hegelianism of the right, a Heideggerianism of the left and a Heideggerianism of the right, a Nietzscheanism of the right and Nietzscheanism of the left, and even . . . a Marxism of the right and a Marxism of the left.[2]

Again, that seems an eminently defensible position to take. If we did not separate work and life then the study of not just philosophy but the arts in general would be much impoverished. Many figures and works would have to be discarded on ideological grounds, and although there are cases where that could be justified (Richard Wagner still divides opinion amongst music lovers given his widely publicised antisemitic views and popularity with major figures in the Nazi movement), it could very easily get out of hand. Derrida's argument that there has to be give and take on such issues is very sensible indeed, and describes what happens with most of those who engage with such material. We are able to deal with the ideas and the narratives in at least a relatively compartmentalised way, recognising that the past really is a different country and that it would be anachronistic to impose our own beliefs on it beyond a certain point; although where that point might lie would be an acceptable topic for debate (as certainly happens with Wagner, whose music was effectively banned in Israel for decades and is still highly controversial there, despite a few concert performances of late). Whether that is also true of the very recent past is, however, another issue, especially with memories of the war still in many people's minds, as they were in the 1980s. It is in that context where Lyotard's critique is situated.

Lyotard and the Sin of Forgetting

Lyotard does not feel able to absolve Heidegger's ideas from the facts of Heidegger's life. His contention is that, as a philosopher, Heidegger has a duty to defend and promote difference rather than to side with those actively working to suppress it, as there is no question the Nazis

86

were doing. Philosophers are under an obligation to do so as far as Lyotard is concerned, otherwise they are in danger of turning themselves into mere 'intellectuals', available to be drafted in to serve the needs of the ruling authorities when required. Heidegger becomes a test case of the philosopher who failed to respect the difference between philosophers and intellectuals, and Lyotard can only be critical of the damage that can lead to in the hands of an unscrupulous grand narrative like Nazism (although Lyotard is no fan of philosophers and intellectuals who allow themselves to be seduced by any grand narrative at all). Lyotard's point is that one can never really forget one's actions, especially those with such recent socio-political prominence, only choose to ignore them, and that is a reaction that cannot be forgiven. 'Forgetting' is being used with heavy irony by Lyotard, making Heidegger sound like an even more reprehensible individual, as if collusion on his scale could ever escape one's memory or fail to prompt some kind of public response; the forgetting has to be seen as deliberate and calculated. Lyotard would seem to be accusing Heidegger of an attitude of indifference to his past, which compounds the sin: Nazism is not a movement which one can be politically or emotionally neutral about. Philosophical politics demands remorse at the very least at such points, and Heidegger provided scant evidence of this.

Heidegger might have been forgiven for remaining silent about the actions of the Nazi regime if he had remained a private citizen with no connection to the party. Many Germans just kept their heads down and got on with their lives, aware of how helpless they were in the face of a totalitarian state with a ruthlessly efficient secret police ready to pounce on even the merest hint of opposition. Even if such a mass of individuals could also be accused in the post-war period of the sin of forgetting, their failure to oppose the Nazi regime can be understood when the penalties for doing so were most likely either death or being sent to a concentration camp. The strong leader principle brooked no dissent at all, promoting a culture of fear that helps to explain the paucity of opposition. When active collusion comes on the scene, however, as it did with Heidegger, then the situation changes and forgiveness has to be withheld by a critic like Lyotard, who is not willing to look for reasons, as Derrida (amongst various other French thinkers in the Heidegger Affair) was, to sanction the continued use of Heidegger's ideas. While Lyotard affirms that '[o]ne must admit the importance and the greatness of Heidegger's thought' and the undoubted influence it has had on his own, he cannot let the matter rest there.[3] He feels the need to keep worrying away about what

Heidegger's career means in both philosophical and political terms, and it clearly poses a problem for his understanding of philosophical politics. Lyotard is too subtle a thinker to conflate Heidegger's life and works, but perhaps there is an unspoken assumption in his writings on the philosopher that there is something there that merits investigation. In some sense Heidegger must be judged, otherwise Lyotard's vision of philosophy as a means of disrupting grand narratives would lose its force. If nothing else, Heidegger's involvement in the establishment of Nazism as the dominant hegemony in German life post-1933 makes him something of a test case for Lyotard's theories on the nature of justice. 'How to judge Martin Heidegger?' could almost be a subtitle to *Heidegger and "the jews"*, because that is what lies behind Lyotard's development of the category of 'the jews'. Heidegger takes his place in an infamous line of individuals and institutions, directly or indirectly responsible for discriminatory policies being enacted against vulnerable minorities for the most spurious of reasons, behaviour which for Lyotard must not be allowed to go unchallenged. Lyotard's moralism can be very hard-edged.

Heidegger's relations with the poet Paul Celan, a Holocaust survivor, in the post-war era bring out the differend that inescapably has to come between two figures from the opposite sides of such an immense ideological divide: 'the contradictory and dissonant elements that marked their relationship', as James K. Lyon describes the situation in his study of the two men.[4] They corresponded on a regular basis over a period of years and finally met in 1967, three years before Celan's death. Although he was very influenced by Heidegger's work and drew on his ideas in his own poetic aesthetic, Celan clearly felt deeply troubled by Heidegger's Nazi connections and how to treat him in the aftermath of the war. A figure such as Celan, whose parents had been victims of the Holocaust, was only too painfully aware of what Heidegger was choosing to forget, and separating his work from his life was anything but an easy matter under the circumstances. The situation was further complicated by Heidegger's admiration for Celan's poetry and his offers of support to him, as well as the various requests he made to meet up with the poet that culminated in their 1967 encounter. Other meetings were to follow, but whether that counts in Heidegger's favour is a moot point. It does not seem to have affected Lyotard's judgement of him as someone who is refusing to acknowledge a past that in reality he should be haunted by. If Heidegger ever was, he kept it well hidden. Even Strauss seemed to have misgivings about what support for the Nazis meant in terms of his art, as he continued to argue the case for the performance of the work of Jewish composers such as Felix Mendelssohn with Nazi officials, to the point where he was removed from the presidency of the Reich Music Chamber in 1935. Thereafter he was to be regarded with suspicion by the Nazi regime and that has to stand to his credit – naivete notwithstanding. No such credit can be extended to Heidegger.

Lyotard as Anti-Populist

Right-wing populism thrives on its opposition to difference, blatantly targeting vulnerable minorities such as immigrants and Jews. It is a tactic that has been very effective in the last few years, with anti-immigrant sentiment in particular finding a substantial audience throughout the West, to the extent of playing a significant role in many national elections. Mouffe's left populism, as we have seen, is designed to provide an alternative to this movement, addressing itself to much of that same audience in the hope of capturing their allegiance. Lyotard, however, is never really a fan of mass movements, which can easily develop the character of grand narratives once they start to achieve a degree of political success. The temptation to go on from there can often prove too much to resist, especially if some leader figures start to emerge and see the possibility of building careers out of the movement (as happens more often than not). Little narrative works against the populist impulse and implies a very different kind of political realm, one in which grand narratives have at best very limited room for manoeuvre. Implicit in Lyotard's opposition is the idea that any mass movement on the right runs the risk of morphing into something like Nazism, and any on the left into a Marxist equivalent, almost as if it is in the DNA of populism to develop in that way, with authoritarianism and totalitarianism eventually asserting themselves: 'Stalinism is not the monopoly of the communist parties', as Lyotard and Gilles Deleuze jointly noted in the 1970s.[5]

Populism comes to represent what Lyotard most dislikes in politics: the suppression of dissent. That is why little narratives are set up in an anti-populist manner, for the short rather than the long haul politically. Philosophical politics cannot support any narrative with ambitions stretching into the long term because of its fears of what the populist temperament might do, and there is a wealth of historical evidence that suggests this can often turn out very badly indeed. While it is hard to think of Heidegger, who was a stern and forbidding figure both personally and philosophically ('void of humour', as Lyon has described him),[6] as a populist, he was nevertheless the beneficiary of a populist movement, the ideology of which he was clearly sympathetic towards as it reflected some of his major philosophical preoccupations. Without directly linking Heidegger's work and life, Lyotard's argument is that Heidegger falls short of the requirements of a philosophical politics, which becomes his way of judging his professional peers. The question of whether there is a left or a right Heideggerianism, as Derrida had claimed, is simply irrelevant to Lyotard: it will never be enough to absolve Heidegger from judgement as to his actions. His Nazi career can never be set to one side, or treated as a temporary aberration that can be forgiven if we take into account his contribution to European intellectual life.

Lyotard's thought in general communicates a deep suspicion about mass movements, and he is temperamentally attuned to the small scale in political terms, hence little narratives, pagan attitudes and the refusal to be absorbed into grand narrative schemes of any description. In an era when populism is threatening to swamp the political realm in the West, complete with prejudices and conspiracy theories (such as the Jews still trying to take over the world through their control of the banking system, media, etc., a notion that keeps being revived and seems impervious to reason),[7] Lyotard's anti-populism provides a model of how to challenge the scapegoating techniques of such movements. To allow oneself to be swept up by populism's one-sided, often hysterically pitched rhetoric is to become complicit with all that proceeds to happen in its name – and that almost invariably will involve making life difficult for 'the jews'.

Scapegoating and 'the jews'

In Lyotard's formulation 'the jews' have always been with us, and that says some very depressing things about the kind of culture we have developed. The Holocaust represents that tendency magnified to a level where society at large can no longer ignore it. Not enough, however, to eliminate antisemitism, which continues to be a factor in Western political life – indeed one that seems to have increased in intensity in recent years (even within establishment political parties such as Labour in the UK). Scapegoating does seem to be a constant element in our history, a component part of grand narratives, even, sad to say, those professing to be based on Enlightenment principles.

The postmodern critique of the Enlightenment project, and its human-ist credentials, draws on just such inconsistencies to make its point. Humanism does not always mean respecting the rights of others when it comes to immigrant groups, especially when their culture is radically different from the nation state where they are trying to settle; it should, yet differends are just as likely to occur in an ostensibly humanist con-text as anywhere else, scapegoating likewise, and 'the jews' constitute a ready-made target when such occasions arise.

Lyotard's notion of 'the jews' has not gone unchallenged, with criticism having been levelled at him for assuming an equivalence between the Jewish race and other minority groups in Western cul-ture. Lyotard can be turned against himself in this instance, with the claim being that the Holocaust alone creates a differend between the Jews and others, not to mention a long history of repression and violence against this one particular group that scandalously enough continues to be added to into our own time (with Holocaust denial to be thrown into the mix for good measure). Victor J. Seidler, for example, argues that '[t]he distinction Lyotard makes between real Jews and "the jews" cannot be sustained. It serves to silence a Jewish tradition which it needs to listen to'.[8] For Ioan Davies, meanwhile, his conception of the Jews is at best 'abstract', that of a philosopher rather than a sociologist or historian.[9] Neal Curtis bluntly calls the use of 'the jews' a 'mistake' and suggests that it would be better, par-ticularly given Jewish treatment of the Palestinians, to change it to '"the homeless" to register such exclusionary practice'.[10]

It would seem unfair to suggest that Lyotard is intending in any way to be disrespectful to Judaism and the Jewish race, however, or playing down the horror of the Holocaust; he would hardly be so concerned to condemn Heidegger's 'forgetfulness' were that the case. Elsewhere he speaks of the hyphen 'in the expression Judeo-Christian' as being situ-ated between 'perhaps the most impenetrable abyss in Western thought' and wonders whether it represents an attempt to suppress Judaism at the expense of Christianity (with no less a figure than St Paul as the instiga-tor of the strategy).[11] Christianity could then be said to be founded on 'the abjection of the Jews', a provocative line of argument that indicates Lyotard fully recognises the desperate plight of the Jewish people over the two millennia of Christian history.[12] Geoffrey Bennington has even argued that 'it could plausibly be claimed that all of Lyotard's thinking is enthralled by questions of Judaism and Jewishness'.[13] At worst the move from Jews to 'the jews' is an arguably rather clumsy (some might even say sensationalist) attempt to make an important point about the

91

sheer extent of social discrimination and prejudice that is to be found in Western history. Scapegoating is deeply engrained there and showing no signs of diminishing; there is always some vulnerable group for the bigoted to pick on. Lyotard is clearly aware of the emotional resonance that the term 'Jews' carries with it in Western culture and of his read-ers' likely knowledge of the Jewish race's feelings of 'abjection' at their treatment, which he is probably taking for granted. In further defence of his line of argument, what he is asking us to recognise is that any of us is capable of acting in a prejudicial way and that at its extreme comes antisemitism and the Holocaust, surely valid points to make in the context of the Heidegger Affair. Yet the reaction of commentators such as Seidler and Davies indicates how difficult it is for anyone claim-ing to judge without criteria to be taken seriously, as if it were just a case of being iconoclastic for its own sake without having any sense of cultural values. These are complaints regularly made against postmod-ernists and poststructuralists by the academic establishment.

Not surprisingly perhaps, Lyotard's relativism can be seen as alien-ating, with Chris Rojek and Bryan S. Turner even wondering whether there is a 'latent amorality' to be noted in his philosophical position.[14] Again, I think that is not the most fair of accusations, being one that could be made against any sceptic putting the relativist case within a debate. To lack a grand narrative to fall back upon is to leave one-self vulnerable as a theorist in that respect, especially when it comes to socially highly sensitive matters like the Holocaust. The fact that Lyotard strives so hard to surmount such difficulties has to be a mark in his favour; his is a socially conscious relativism and, as indicated before, I think there is a strong case to be made for him as a moralist.

Heidegger Post-Lyotard

The Heidegger Affair remains topical right into the new century, with thinkers still debating and worrying over how to judge his Nazi history and its effect on his philosophy, as other material from that period (lectures and seminars, for example) is coming to be published and translated. Donatella Di Cesare, for example, follows on from Farías and Lyotard in emphasising the depth of Heidegger's commit-ment to the Nazi cause, and finding disturbing links between his anti-semitism and philosophical theories. Heidegger's 'Black Notebooks' from the 1930s and 40s reveal him to be yet another exponent of scapegoating, regarding the Jews as being in the vanguard of moder-nity, a cultural phenomenon to which Heidegger was vehemently opposed.[15] He is to be categorised as an exponent of 'metaphysical antisemitism', which for Di Cesare 'is more abstract and at the same time more dangerous than a simple aversion to Jews and Judaism', because it led to Heidegger accusing the Jews of trying to bring about 'the oblivion of Being'.[16] In other words, his antisemitism is deeply embedded in his philosophical thought, where the nature of Being is the central concern, hence 'his obstinate silence' in the post-war years.[17] For Elliot R. Wolfson, however, the issue is more complicated in that he detects the influence of Jewish mysticism on Heidegger's thought, Wolfson himself being a noted scholar of that aspect of Jewish culture.[18] Intriguing though that undoubtedly is, enough for Wolfson to claim that Heidegger's work transcends questions of anti-semitism, one suspects it would not have altered Lyotard's opinion of the philosopher, any more than Heidegger's relations with Paul Celan could. The collusion with Nazism remains, pre-empting any benefit of the doubt.

It would be a matter of no small import were Heidegger's philosophy to be encoded with Nazi ideology and if that is what his concept of Being entails, as many are now convinced, then it would become very difficult indeed to defend his work – or teach it without reference to its socio-political context either. Tom Rockmore for one is adamant that Heidegger has to be judged in just such a fashion:

> Examination of Heidegger's corpus shows that Heidegger's Nazism, real and ideal, is a permanent feature of his thought beginning in 1933. To fail to take his Nazism into account in the interpretation of his philosophical and 'postphilosophical' thought, to endeavor to be more friendly to Heidegger than to the truth, is finally to distance oneself from the concern with truth.[19]

Other recent commentators, such as Emmanuel Faye and Adam Knowles, follow up this line of argument, identifying an explicitly Nazi cast to Heidegger's thought and teaching in the 1930s and 40s.[20] Not everyone is as willing to see a 'smoking gun' revealing such a link, however, and no doubt the debate will continue, further dividing opinion within the philosophical profession in the process. Lyotard's approach to Heidegger is in many ways more subtle in that he does not go too deeply into this particular issue, putting forward other reasons for criticising him, mainly his retreat into silence and to all intents and purposes into forgetting his Nazi past. There is no need to pore over various interpretations of Being, or to ponder their implications in ideological terms; Lyotard's point is a moral one that goes beyond such considerations, which may never be satisfactorily resolved anyway. Left and right Heideggerians are likely to keep on emerging in future philosophical debate as his era recedes.

Lyotard's stance on Heidegger remains highly relevant, therefore, in a society in which antisemitism is still a major cultural problem (with Holocaust denial still attracting considerable support) and in which scapegoating of vulnerable minorities has all but become public policy in many Western nations. His point is that antisemitism and scapegoating are part of the same cultural phenomenon, a disposition towards discrimination that ideologies are only too prone to encourage and that his philosophical thinking is expressly designed to oppose. Forgetting remains a blot on our culture, and Heidegger has great symbolic significance in that respect: a figure whose career cannot help but invite the attention of a philosophical politics. As usual with Lyotard, it is the political aspect that takes precedence. Ultimately, what is at stake is the nature of the responsibility that philosophers have, both to their subject and to the public, and from Lyotard's perspective Heidegger has signally failed to uphold this. The larger point that is being made, however, and one that goes well beyond Heidegger, is that grand narratives are quite shameless at forgetting whatever they happen to find inconvenient; whatever that is will just be erased from the record, as colonised countries know only too well. That is what Lyotard is warning us we should always be on the lookout for (and with populism in the ascendant we very much need to be) and what little narratives are set up to expose.

Notes

1. See, for example, Moffitt, *The Global Rise of Populism*.
2. Derrida, *The Ear of the Other*, p. 32.
3. Lyotard, *'Heidegger and "the jews"'*: A Conference, pp. 135–47 (p. 138).
4. Lyon, *Paul Celan and Martin Heidegger*, p. viii.
5. Lyotard (with Gilles Deleuze), 'Concerning the Vincennes Psychoanalysis Department', in *Political Writings*, pp. 68–9 (p. 68).
6. Lyon, *Paul Celan and Martin Heidegger*, p. 1.
7. The claims made by the infamous *Protocols of the Elders of Zion*, which continue to be deployed by antisemites, and the text to be sold. It can be found on the Amazon website, for example.
8. Seidler, 'Identity, Memory and Difference', in Rojek and Turner, *The Politics of Jean-François Lyotard*, pp. 102–27 (p. 124).
9. Davies, 'Narrative, Knowledge and Art', in ibid., pp. 84–101 (p. 100).

10. Curtis, *Against Autonomy*, p. 163.
11. Lyotard and Gruber, *The Hyphen*, p. 13. Gruber's reply takes issue with Lyotard's reading of the hyphen as the disclosure of a differend (with the Christian side intent on dominating the Judaic, therefore not bearing witness), arguing instead that 'it is also here the sign of a crossing that bears fruit' (ibid., p. 54). Whereas the hyphen signals a separation for Lyotard, for Gruber it is a union. As the work's translators point out, it is a punctuation mark worth having a philosophical debate about, because what is at stake is 'the nature of the Judeo-Christian connection . . . one of the oldest and most important debates in the West' (ibid., p. vii).
12. Ibid., p. 22.
13. Bennington, *Late Lyotard*, p. 66.
14. Rojek and Turner, 'Introduction', in *The Politics of Jean-François Lyotard*, p. 3.
15. See Heidegger, *Ponderings II-VI*, *Ponderings VII-XI* and *Ponderings XII-XV*.
16. Di Cesare, *Heidegger and the Jews*, p. ix.
17. Ibid., p. 4.
18. Wolfson, *The Duplicity of Philosophy's Shadow*.
19. See Rockmore, *On Heidegger's Nazism and Philosophy*, pp. 300–1.
20. See Faye, *Heidegger*, and Knowles, *Heidegger's Fascist Affinities*.

Chapter 6

Thinking the Politics of the Future

In the last years of his career Lyotard's attention turned to techno-capitalism, which he felt was operating against the best interests of the human race, being motivated solely by considerations of profit and having no commitment to ethical values. This is the concern of one of his most provocative works, *The Inhuman*, which, looking ahead to the future and the eventual death of our sun, speculates about how the corporate sector might respond to this catastrophic event by developing AI systems that could survive the extinction of humanity.[1] Were that to happen, it would represent a move into the inhuman, which Lyotard argues we should be preparing ourselves to resist: 'what else remains as "politics" except resistance to this inhuman?'.[2] Since the early 1990s, when the book was published, technological progress has mushroomed and there is an increasing sense of public unease about what the development of AI, and the robotics industry that has grown out of this so rapidly in recent years, could mean for the future of humanity. Lyotard's work on this topic looks extremely prescient and his value to current debates in the area invites reassessment.

Of Cyborgs and Cybernetic Systems

The inhuman is looking more and more like the face of the future and not necessarily the very distant future either, given the huge amount of resource that is being poured into robotics research as well as the very substantial financial benefits it offers to bring to the corporate sector – benefits that many companies are already reaping by replacing staff with robots (as in the case of Amazon warehouses). If that is our fate, then it raises some very awkward questions about corporate power and how to challenge the undoubted dominance that it has in our culture, especially when allied to techno-science; awkward questions too about where humanity fits into all of this, if at all. Do we lose some of our humanity if we have to interact with robots and AI systems on a regular basis? Questions like that need to be asked, and Lyotard poses two key ones to get *The Inhuman* under way: 'what if human beings, in humanism's sense, were in the process of, constrained into, becoming inhuman (that's the first part)? And (the second part), what if what is "proper" to human-kind were to be inhabited by the inhuman?'.[3] Donna Haraway may have been excited by the prospect of the inhuman coming to inhabit the domain of the human in the form of cyborgs ('The machine is not an it to be animated, worshipped, and dominated. The machine is us, our processes, an aspect of our embodiment'),[4] and more recently James Lovelock has expressed similar pro-cyborg views, but one wonders what Lyotard would make of all this. Lovelock can in fact sound quite apocalyptic about the coming of cyborgs, asserting in an interview that 'I think the chemical-physical type of humanity has had its time. We've mucked about with the planet and we're moving towards a systems type of thing, [a future spe-cies] running on cybernetics'.[5] This will be the age of what his latest book calls the 'Novacene'.[6] Cybernetics is, of course, the business of techno-science, so we do not have to wait until the death of the sun before recognising the necessity of monitoring the sector's exploits very carefully, especially given the fascination it holds for the cor-porate world, which is always quick in latching on to technological advances. The notion of the human coming to be replaced by sys-tems would represent a victory for the inhuman of precisely the kind that Lyotard is determined to resist.

Lyotard's work on this topic therefore makes an excellent start-ing point from which to extend the debate about AI. He is often described as anti-humanist in outlook, as are many other postmod-ernist and poststructuralist thinkers because of their opposition to the Enlightenment project and the humanism that evolved out of that (part of the 'new conservativism', too, in their suspicion of rea-son, as Jürgen Habermas has argued).[7] For such thinkers, human-ism has become part of the ruling ideology in the West and is to be considered suspect on that basis, its values all too often shown up as hypocritical. Yet for all the criticism of humanism that he expresses in the work, the nature of Lyotard's arguments in *The Inhuman* makes it possible for them to be used by humanist-oriented think-ers too. Not all of the latter deserve to be dismissed as hypocritical, and they would be very concerned indeed at the need to preserve what is 'proper' to humanity, even if they might characterise this somewhat differently to Lyotard (although I take the point made by Matthew R. McLennan that it is 'Humanity' that Lyotard is taking the side of, rather than humanism as it is traditionally understood).[8] Once again, it is the tactical side of Lyotard's analysis that needs to be emphasised. It is corporate power that he is critiquing, and one does not have to be an anti-humanist to engage in that enterprise, not now that the corporate sector has come to dominate so much of our existence through its control of the technological realm. The hegemony of that sector is hard to deny, and many are quite understandably uneasy about it, wondering just how far techno-science might choose to go in marginalising humanity in promoting the cause of the inhuman. As a chapter title to Alison Dagnes' book on the polarisation of politics in recent times pithily puts it: 'Money + Tech = Problems'.[9]

The enemy that we are faced with as Lyotard sees it is 'development', which is interested only in efficiency: 'Development imposes the saving of time. To go fast is to forget fast, to retain only the information that is useful afterwards, as in "rapid reading"'.[10] Development is what capitalism has always been obsessed by, the urge to grow and expand, to open up new markets and to deliver its products with the greatest efficiency possible in order to increase profit margins; it proceeds 'according to its internal dynamic alone', which makes it a formidable opponent.[11] Neither development nor capitalism actually belongs to anyone or to any particular state; they are diffuse phenomena breaching national boundaries and are thus very difficult to pin down or check all that successfully (as multinationals have long since realised to their advantage). Even the avowedly anti-capitalist Soviet Union went in for development in a big way (as Jean Baudrillard's point about the dominance of production in communist regimes emphasised),[12] hence its many elaborate and generally wildly over-ambitious 'Five Year Plans' for both industry and agriculture. After the fall of that system capitalism quickly resumed operation there too, complete with its more efficient form of development. From the Industrial Revolution onwards, the human cost of keeping that system going has never been a great concern of development. It is in the performance of the system and the profits that flow from it that its real interest lies, and it can be very single-minded, even ruthless, in following it up, treating cultural norms as there to be broken. To that extent, the inhuman is already an intrinsic part of the process, and Lyotard's understandable fear is that it will become ever more pronounced as AI's potential to outlive humanity is recognised. Basically, development is not to be trusted. As he notes elsewhere:

development comes to upset the human plan of emancipation. We have signs of this in the harmful effects of the most developed civilizations, effects motivating the ecology movement, the endless reforms in education, the proliferation of ethics commissions, the crackdown on drug trafficking, and so on.[13]

While Lyotard is a critic of humanist plans of emancipation in general, his comments signal that development is a law unto itself, as much of a threat to humanists as anti-humanists – an ironic point to make given that development is a product of humanism's drive towards emancipation. What development has proved to be very adept at doing, however, is co-opting the language of humanist emancipation for its own devious ends – ends that are anything but emancipatory in intent. Development is capable of almost endless cynicism in that respect.

The world of AI is the world of complex patterns determined by algorithms, which increasingly drive the systems on which humanity depends, from public utilities through to stock markets; none of us can escape their influence on our lives. Their function seems to be to overcome events and the unharmonisability that to Lyotard is what constitutes the reality of human existence. Algorithms give an appearance of control, therefore, but only that. The everyday world, where events and the sublime can disrupt human planning at any point, has to be considered unalgorithmable; AI can only have an impact on it by creating an alternative reality. Events, however, fall into no discernible pattern. Algorithms are a harbinger of the inhuman to come, and the more that development deploys them the more worried we ought to be; preferring algorithms to the human has far-reaching political implications that a thinker like Lyotard has to oppose. He could hardly condone the human being turned into a system in the cybernetic sense. Development must not be given free rein to carry out its programme.

'Can Thought Go On Without a Body?'

Descartes believed that thought could go on without a body (insisting on 'the total difference between mind and body', the latter being for him essentially just a 'machine'),[14] and generations of philosophy students have debated the issue as part of their studies, although in a fairly abstract fashion. But the notion has become considerably more relevant since the advent of AI and that is what prompts Lyotard's

99

intervention in 'Can Thought Go On Without a Body?'. It is one of the more challenging pieces of writing in his oeuvre, one whose over-lapping arguments and constant shifts of direction can give rise to a wide range of readings. Some of it is true, some of it is speculation (quite wild at that), but its underlying unease about the increasing power of a techno-scientific driven development is well worth airing, even if Lyotard chooses some extreme examples to get us to think through the implications of this. James Williams sees the piece as an example of Lyotard's 'postmodern irony', a style that he deploys frequently in his later career.[15] It is a debate between two voices, 'He' and 'She', about the prospects for humanity in the face of the eventual extinction of life in the solar system – and, crucially, how the corporate sector might respond to this event. 'He' is deeply pes-simistic about what this will mean for humankind, suggesting that the corporate world's obsession with performance will dispose it to make ever more extensive use of computerised systems because they offer a higher level of efficiency and reliability than the human; systems do exactly what their programmes tell them to, lacking the capacity for unpredictability that humans always carry within them. The development model will always gravitate towards the inhuman for that reason, as it has been doing for quite some time now, replac-ing human beings with automated systems in a wide range of areas: first there were machines, now robots and AI systems powered by algorithms. It is a deeply pessimistic view of the world that is offered in the piece and it can make the task of resistance seem more of a doomed gesture than anything else (would cyborgs resist, one won-ders?). It is, as Lyotard puts it, all that remains for us to do faced with this desperate situation, but there is no suggestion that its success can be guaranteed – at best, we are only delaying development's progress. Admittedly, that progress will eventually come up against the death of the sun, and it is at least possible that it will fail to overcome this event, regardless of how much research it devotes to the problem; but that is hardly much consolation to humanity, apparently condemned to find ways to cope with development's relentless 'internal dynamic' in the interim. It is a distinctly dystopian vision overall, and even if the death of the sun will not be a factor for an almost unimaginably long time, the intrusion of a development-led AI into our lives is here right now and it will not stop of its own accord.

Jeanette Winterson's novel *Frankisstein* takes the conflict between the human and the inhuman that AI poses for us as its theme, treat-ing it as a contemporary version of Mary Shelley's *Frankenstein*.

Winterson's inventor character Victor Stein is a visionary along the lines of Shelley's protagonist, this time propounding the virtues of AI, which he does with an evangelical zeal as an inescapable consequence of our historical development. He breaks human history into three phases, '*Life: Evolution-based*', '*Life: Partially self-designing*' and '*Life: Fully self-designing*', arguing the merits of moving from the second phase (where humanity is currently placed) into the third, where AI will be dominant, with no need for any interaction with humanity.[16] There is a chilling tone to his rationale for developing as quickly as possible into that state (effectively Lovelock's Novacene), telling an audience at a lecture he is delivering that 'artificial intelligence is not sentimental – it is biased towards best possible outcomes. The human race is not a best possible outcome'.[17] It is precisely that kind of mindset that 'He' is so worried about, and AI's real-life advocates can sound just as enthusiastic as Victor Stein about the prospect of that third phase, talking disparagingly, as Stein does too, about the body as 'meat' and consciousness as an entity that can, and should, be detached from it in order to maximise its potential.[18] For such zealots as these, thought without a body is a condition much to be wished for and that cannot come about soon enough. Development as Lyotard conceives of it is as unsentimental as Stein is as well about working towards its interpretation of the best possible outcomes, and as little concerned with what it would mean for the human race to be overtaken by a 'fully self-designing' AI. Frankenstein's creation of a 'Modern Prometheus' proves to be a dead end. The creature is doomed to perish on the icecap after he springs from the ship that has rescued his inventor and allows himself to be 'borne away by the waves, and lost in darkness and distance', but an AI Prometheus is unlikely to make things so easy for humanity.[19] Human beings are sentimental and they do have emotions, characteristics that are absolutely fundamental to their sense of humanity, as are their bodies, giving them every reason to fear what their fate may be at the hands of an unsentimental, potentially planet-dominating, self-designing AI. The Novacene is an ominous threat hanging over us as a species.

Not all AI enthusiasts envisage such an unsentimental, anti-human style of AI. The mathematician Marcus du Sautoy, for example, thinks that we are beginning to see the emergence of 'an empathetic AI, which understands what it means to be human'.[20] Whether a self-designing AI would find it useful to continue to be so is another point entirely; it may well decide there is nothing much to be gained from doing so and pursue outcomes which could be against humanity's best interests. Understanding what it means to be human could easily lead to AI systems choosing to exert control over us, co-opting us into their plans, or perhaps even just to give up on us altogether as beings biologically hampered by being trapped in our bodies. Du Sautoy feels that we should look on the bright side and see AI as 'a powerful collaborative tool' we could use to make our lives easier, claiming that 'there is far too much fear around this subject'.[21] But if life is going to be reduced to a question of mere outcomes then humanity might turn out to be the one that ends up 'lost in darkness and distance'. That is the fear that 'He' is expressing: the Novacene pushed to its logical limits and humanity having become superfluous to its new species.

'She' adopts a notably more optimistic tone than 'He' does, however, introducing the issue of gender into the discussion and arguing that this should be built into the machines designed to outlive the death of our solar system: 'Your thinking machines will have to be nourished not just on radiation but on the irremediable differend of gender'.[22] It is a provocative argument designed to introduce an element of the human into AI, although it is unlikely to be one that would sway the minds of the AI and robotics industry, where efficiency and performance are the only characteristics that are considered important. Reducing the level of human involvement is always going to exert a strong appeal in the profit-obsessed corporate sector, which would consider the issue of gender a mere distraction from its primary concerns. 'She's' argument also brings the notion of a gender differend into the discussion, inviting us to consider its implications for dealing with the adverse impact of the inhuman on our society.[23] The inhuman simply rides roughshod over issues such as gender, being entirely oriented towards performance and efficiency, which are perceived in strictly mechanical terms. Difference and diversity are of no interest to the inhuman; indeed, that is what renders it inhuman to a thinker like Lyotard, for whom difference and diversity are the most vital aspects of our social existence, to be defended with all the philosophical ability he can muster. That would be his version of a best possible outcome. What 'She's' monologue brings out, despite the critical importance of gender and her impassioned defence of it ('Finally, the human body has a gender. It's an accepted proposition that sexual difference is a paradigm of an incompleteness of not just bodies, but minds too . . . The notion of gender dominant in contemporary society wants this gap closed'),[24] is just how unlikely it is that it will play any significant part in the thinking of those in charge of development. Profit-making has no need of it – except in the trivial sense of naming personal assistant robots Alexa, which is hardly an example of an 'irremediable differend' at work. Alexa is only the beginning of where the search for AI's best possible outcomes will lead and they will not always require the involvement of, or commands from, humanity. Nor need AI systems always feel under any obligation to understand us, or to treat us empathetically; pursuing their goals will take precedence instead.

Whether thought can go on without a body depends on whether AI can be considered to think in the human sense of the term. In Cartesian dualism the assumption is that thought can go on without a body since thinking is the dominant partner in the mind-body relationship, the factor that defines us as human and differentiates us from the animal kingdom. Thought continuing in this respect is akin to the soul surviving the body, so from a religious standpoint this is an acceptable argument (atheists would of course demur). What Victor Stein and his counterparts in the AI industry mean by thought, however, is sophisticated algorithmic programming with the ability to go on programming itself without the need for any human intervention, precisely what Lyotard feels transports us into the realm of the inhuman. Perhaps the final answer to the question is that inhuman thought could go on without a body, since the body is merely a contingent extra to AI. That is not, however, a situation which is likely to be much to the benefit of humanity.

Corporate Power and Robot Labour

The Inhuman presents a warning to us about what the grand narrative of corporate power might choose to do with the AI that will increasingly be at its disposal, already more of an issue than it was when the book came out (in technological terms the early 1990s can seem like the distant past, so fast do things move in this area) and destined to be so into the indefinite future. The generalised sense of public disquiet, and even mistrust, about where this is all heading is not difficult to understand, and it will become ever more of an issue with every technological improvement that comes on stream; it will take more than using gendered names for machines to overcome that (gender in a cyborg world would be an interesting subject to contemplate as well). What is always worrying in such cases is the lack of consideration that is given to the factor of the human, as if technological change just has to be accepted regardless of its effect on the public realm, that it is an end in itself that must not be tampered with or restricted in any way. It is rather like the early days of industrialisation when a way of life was simply destroyed by the wholesale introduction of the factory system, with the human impact it was having (on health and general living standards) largely discounted by the perpetrators of the change, who were firmly focused on production to the exclusion of all else. In each case everything was subsumed under the narrative of the technology, which was allowed to take precedence over any other considerations. Humanity was supposed to adapt to the technology, not the other way round; the internal dynamic demanded it and that is surely describable as an example of the inhuman in action. The human is little more than an afterthought from that perspective, something to be constrained into acceptance of a technological takeover, as the working class forcibly was over the course of the nineteenth century.

We stand on the verge of a similar destruction now in terms of the reduction of employment opportunities as a result of the wholesale shift over to automated production processes backed up by robot labour. This is the line argued by the economic historian Carl Benedikt Frey in his book *The Technology Trap*, where he is highly critical of the development imperative, arguing that '[t]hough it is often taken as a given, there is no fundamental reason why technological ingenuity should be allowed to thrive'.[25] Unfortunately enough, however, that is generally what happens, as if it was preordained to be that way and that any opposition to continual 'progress' is to be dismissed as wrong-headed (quite possibly mere nostalgia for a lost past, as the greens and no-growth movements are so often accused of displaying). Money + Tech engaged in devising self-designing AI = Very Significant Existential Problems.

Robot labour has been working its way up from manual to far more skilled occupations and procedures, progressively diminishing human input as it goes: medicine is a case in point, which raises the unappealing prospect of being diagnosed and treated by an algorithm (well on the way to being an inhuman encounter, quite a few of us would think). The same argument is trotted out each time: that it saves on costs, which in effect means that it increases corporate profits because staffing can be cut – often very substantially. Profit and the inhuman go together quite naturally: robots do not strike, nor do they demand higher wages and better working conditions, meaning that there is no need for holidays, sickness pay, maternity leave, pension plans, etc. As far as most managements go, that makes them all but perfect employees, even better than cyborgs presumably; unpalatable though it may be even to contemplate such a possibility, companies are much easier to run when you remove the human factor (this is not intended to be an argument in robots' favour, just a reflection of the managerial outlook). What form resistance should take in these circumstances is not at all clear, however; technophobia alone is not the answer, although it would be only too easy for the left to fall into that trap (as some do). Indeed, the general historical picture of development can encourage a technophobic response, as can be seen in Frey's analysis. It is an issue destined to have a huge impact on our political life for the foreseeable future; job security, for example, tends to vanish in the wake of the robot invasion for a significant proportion of the general population. The gig economy is where that will lead for more and more of the workforce, although even that may see cutbacks. Drones are already taking over some of the delivery process, and that is a trend that can only increase as things stand – not much in the way of collaborative activity taking place there. The employment market has certainly come to be inhabited by the inhuman, and human beings look likely to become ever more disadvantaged in consequence. Something along the lines of a 'back to the human' campaign is worth considering – and that is not just a case of technophobia. The notion of introducing a universal living wage for human beings, irrespective of whether they have any employment to supplement it, has come in for a certain amount of consideration in recent years, with some short-term trial runs even being attempted (in Finland, for example).[26] But one can well imagine how unpopular that would be with the corporate sector, as it will only be made possible by taxing them to cover the gap between an assumed human labour force's tax return and the predominantly robot working force they will be increasingly likely to have. Nor will it be popular with right-wing governments, which are traditionally committed to low-tax regimes as well as constitutionally opposed to providing support for those without employment: the world most certainly does not owe you a living as far as the former are concerned. Some interesting confrontations no doubt loom on such issues.

It may have sounded rather like a science fiction tale in Lyotard, and as Ashley Woodward rightly remarks we do have to bear in mind the fabular quality of this piece ('the fable of the "solar catastrophe"').[27] Yet the way that AI is developing by taking over so many areas of human interaction makes the idea of a deliberately engineered marginalisation of the human by the AI and robotics sector seem all too plausible – and all too likely to induce a sense of deep melancholy in the face of the existential crisis that it is generating. Whether that deliberate bypassing of humanity would, or could, go to the lengths that Lyotard suggests in 'He's' monologue is debatable (although a strikingly attention-grabbing way of putting it), but the clash of interests between the human and the inhuman is already shaping up as an area of immense importance in the way that our culture develops: one that Lyotard was right to highlight in such emotive terms in order to bring home to us the seriousness of the cultural change that it is signalling. How we adapt, and indeed whether we can adapt, to AI will test humanity's resilience for generations to come. Whether you are humanist or anti-humanist you would have to find this a matter of considerable concern: anti-humanists no more wish to see humanity marginalised than humanists do, nor to see thought reduced to algorithmic patterns. There is a certain air of 'melancholia' about Lyotard's analysis that Williams notes, which has become something of a characteristic of leftist thought in recent years: a recognition that there are no simple solutions to putting things right, particularly when Marxism's decline is taken into account.[28] Politically, the left gives an impression of being in retreat, a difficult condition to overcome once it sets in, especially when it sees the gains it has fought for so vigorously over the years – workers' rights, generous welfare provision, etc. – being systematically cut back by right-wing governments. Recovering some of that lost ground is about as high as leftist aspirations can go at present – and even that that can seem overly ambitious in the current political climate.

Enzo Traverso has some perceptive comments to make about this phenomenon of 'left melancholy', arguing that 'the end of communism has broken [the] dialectic between past and future' on which belief in Marxism depended: that is, the link between theory and practice, between what the theory promised and what the practice actually had been delivering.[29] Given such a debilitating loss of belief, and the depressing memories of communism's record that lay behind it (Stalinism as an all too notable example), it becomes necessary 'to rethink the history of socialism and Marxism through the prism of melancholy', which does sound very much like what Lyotard was trying to do when he acknowledged a differend between himself and Pierre Souyri in the aftermath of his Pouvoir Ouvrier days.[30] The effect of communism's collapse on the left has been dramatic: 'The tension between past and future becomes a kind of "negative", mutilated dialectic. In such a context, we discover a melancholic vision of history as remembrance of the vanquished'.[31] Traverso wants the left to face up to this and move on past our melancholy and feelings of defeat to reconstruct the struggle that has to take place if neoliberalism is to be reined in. We must resist any lapse into defeatism, which is easier said than done when it is not just neoliberalism that is the enemy to be countered but fascism and right-wing extremism in general too (to which list we can add the spectre of self-designing AI). Lyotard, however, does not give up; he may be nihilistic but he is never defeatist.

As to whether the corporate sector would, or even could, go to such extremes as 'He's' pessimism suggests, we only have to consider its continued heavy reliance on the products of the fossil fuel industry, which the vast majority of the science profession has made clear will wreck the planet if we go on using these fuels as we are doing for much longer. Or that one of the responses to that desperate state of affairs is to plan how we might be able to colonise other planets, such as Mars, after we have trashed our own: anything other than change our ways here to prevent such an outcome, it would seem. There is no doubt that the corporate sector would benefit hugely if such a programme were ever launched in earnest; in fact, the beginnings of it are already in place, initiating yet another round of technical ingenuity (Mars missions are being seriously considered by several parties). This means that development all but has a vested interest in the destruction of the environment to necessitate space colonisation (this is pushing it a bit, I agree, but I think that Lyotard wants us to consider worst-case scenarios like this). The social responsibility of the corporate sector leaves just about everything to be desired at such junctures, and it gives little indication of wanting to change its ways – neither will it, as long as profits are forthcoming. (In this context, it is always worth remembering that it was the corporate banking and finance industry that brought Western society to the brink of financial collapse in the 2007–8 credit crash, and that has largely evaded taking responsibility for this event, despite having to be bailed out at huge expense by public funds. We should never underestimate just how far the corporate sector is willing to go in the pursuit of profit; nor expect them to show much remorse at the impact of this process on the public. It should also give us pause for thought that economics commentators are already beginning to warn that it could happen all over again, as the industry has gradually reverted to its old risky practices and the dubious financial 'products' these involved.)

Space colonisation would most likely be the realm of cyborgs, thus a further step into the inhuman as Lyotard would see it. Lovelock's rather offhand comment that 'I always imagine one of these new cyborg-type people standing on a five-bar gate and looking out at the humans' is enough to induce a bout of melancholia in any of us wishing to preserve the human and the values that go along with it.[32] What would it feel like being on the other side of the gate in the gaze of the cyborg observer? I suspect I am not the only one whose heart sinks at such a prospect – and, again, I do not think that is a technophobic attitude.

Sarah Wilson is another commentator to detect a note of melancholia in Lyotard's writings post-1968.[33] 'He' particularly gives that impression, while 'She' is noticeably more upbeat (as the left will have to start being if it wants to garner support for its opposition). It is as if Lyotard is offering us two ways to look at the issue without actually coming down definitively on one side or the other, recognising that they are both expressing legitimate concerns about the nature of development and how to react to it. A more traditional kind of political theorist – a Marxist, say – would come up with a detailed programme of how to curb the corporate sector's power, but that would involve speaking from a specific ideological position, something that Lyotard resolutely avoids in order to steer clear of grand narratives. It is typical of Lyotard to be that careful of being over-directive, the very opposite of what a Marxist would think was necessary in that situation. But he wants us to be aware that we are dealing with an issue that can, and should, be looked at from various standpoints, all of which we might find jostling against each other within our own mind: we all have our internal 'multiplicity of voices' that deserve to be cultivated. Lyotard presents the problem and indicates why it worries him, but he promises no ready solution to it, we have to make our own contribution to the debate and see where that takes us. In effect, it is back to you as a reader to philosophise your way out of the problem, an opportunity to try out some thought experiments of your own devising; Lyotard will provide no easy answers, as that for him would be an authoritarian move. While one can understand why some readers and commentators would find this trait irritating, Lyotard's point is that to be more directive is to stray back into grand narrative territory. But there is no disguising the depth of his concern about development and its devious methods, which have a track record of generating worst-case scenarios for others to clear up.

The End is Nigh

A further point to make about Lyotard's thesis is that catastrophe might not be as far away as he had assumed either. Humankind may well have disappeared long before the sun dies if global warming continues at its current rapid, still largely unchecked (and quite possibly uncheckable) pace: another of development's legacies that we have been left to struggle with and are not doing so with any great sense of conviction. Some of the projections on this are truly scary and suggest that we may be catapulted into the state of the inhuman far earlier than scientists had thought – a few generations rather than several billion years, perhaps, hence Lovelock's enthusiasm for cyborgs. Even since Lyotard's death in 1998 this situation has become radically more alarming, without as yet generating the kind of concerted international response that its seriousness all too clearly demands (by which I mean government intervention rather than just public protests). Meanwhile, development just goes on its merry way, exacerbating the problem by its ever-growing appetite for fossil fuels to power its projects, as well as by generously funding studies to come up with appropriately sceptical conclusions on their environmental impact that climate crisis deniers take as gospel. Except for those deniers, we know what we should be doing, but the will to put it into operation is pointedly lacking (differends, on the other hand, are manifestly not lacking).

Global warming may well be the determinant of when the end is nigh for humankind, but other possible causes could also be cited, if some further speculation might be indulged ('Can Thought Go On Without a Body?' certainly encourages this activity). A massive meteorite strike, which Earth has suffered at various points in the past, could prompt a move into the inhuman if it was destructive enough; for that matter, so could the eruption of a supervolcano such as Yellowstone, which would cause almost unimaginable devastation in North America (with a severe knock-on effect to the rest of the world in time). Scientists have noted that the magnetic north pole has been 'wandering' in recent years and that there is always the possibility that the Earth's magnetic field could flip over (as it appears to have done several times in the distant past) and in the process perhaps weaken enough to expose humanity to the deadly radiation from the solar wind that the field currently protects us from. Such an event could even mean that the planet is stripped of its atmosphere, which very obviously would spell the end of life here.[34] There is also the question of what might happen if there were any significant changes to our galaxy, the Milky Way. We tend to take it for granted that this will remain fairly stable, but we cannot know this will always be the case. The galaxies in the universe are speeding away from each other in a manner that could, some physicists have speculated, lead to a 'big rip', where the universe tears itself apart, although this would be well into the future and past the death of the sun. Another notable exception to the supposed stability of our own galaxy is that a neighbouring galaxy to ours, Andromeda, appears to be heading towards us on a collision course, expected to occur in around 4.5 billion years. Even if computers do survive the death of the sun, they may not be able to survive either of the latter two phenomena; they really would spell doomsday for any development project, for the inhuman as well as the human. In the interim, however, speculation over global warming, very much a 'here and now' problem, gives the pessimists within our ranks more than enough to brood upon. Thinking the politics of the future is not for the faint-hearted, and Lyotard is not going to pretend otherwise.

Notes

1. For a concise summary on current scientific thinking on what the eventual fate of the sun is likely to be, see the note in Woodward, *Lyotard and the Inhuman Condition*, pp. 37–8 (note 4). Lyotard's argument does not, however, depend on the scientific details, being in the nature of a thought experiment on his part.
2. Lyotard, 'Introduction: About the Human', in *The Inhuman*, pp. 1–7 (p. 7).
3. Ibid., p. 3.
4. Haraway, *Simians, Cyborgs, and Women*, p. 180.
5. Vince, 'The Chemical-Physical Type of Humanity Has Had Its Time', pp. 45–7 (p. 47).
6. See Lovelock, *Novacene*.
7. See Habermas, *The New Conservatism*.
8. '[F]or both the later and the earlier Lyotard, the Idea of Humanity is operative, but, precisely, at the expense of a nihilating-transcendent, determinate vision of humanity, as either essence or project . . . As such it is operative at the expense rather than to the benefit of humanism' (McLennan, 'Anthro-Paralogy: Antihumanism in Lyotard's Late Works', in Bickis and Shields, *Re-Reading Jean-François Lyotard*, pp. 43–53 (p. 47)). For all the significant differences, both humanists and anti-humanists share a commitment to some version of 'the Idea of Humanity', which does distinguish them sharply from those seeking to push the cause of the inhuman.
9. Dagnes, *Super Mad at Everything All the Time*, p. 75.
10. Lyotard, *The Inhuman*, p. 3.

11. Ibid., p. 7.
12. See Baudrillard, *The Mirror of Production*.
13. Lyotard and Gruber, *The Hyphen*, p. 5.
14. Descartes, *Philosophical Writings*, pp. 121, 120.
15. Williams, *Lyotard and the Political*, p. 123.
16. Winterson, *Frankissstein*, pp. 72, 73.
17. Ibid., p. 74.
18. For a particularly striking exploration of how this notion might work out in human terms, both in terms of its advantages and drawbacks, see William Gibson's novel *Neuromancer*.
19. Shelley, *Frankenstein*, p. 223.
20. Du Sautoy, 'The Q & A', pp. 6–8 (p. 7).
21. Ibid., p. 8.
22. Lyotard, 'Can Thought Go on Without a Body?', in *The Inhuman*, pp. 8–23 (p. 22).
23. For a discussion of Lyotard's impact on gender studies, see Grebowicz, *Gender After Lyotard*. The collection takes a positive approach to Lyotard's work, although other feminists have been more critical of Lyotard's rejection of narratives of emancipation, regarding these as integral to the campaign for full equality between the sexes (see, for example, the contributors to Nicholson, *Feminism/Postmodernism*). Nancy Fraser and Linda Nicholson argue that Lyotard 'rules out the sort of critical social theory which employs general categories like gender, race, and class' (Fraser and Nicholson, 'Social Criticism Without Philosophy', in ibid., pp. 19–38 (p. 24)).
24. Lyotard, 'Can Thought Go on Without a Body?', pp. 20, 21.
25. Frey, *The Technology Trap*, p. xi.
26. The two-year trial was not renewed by the Finnish government, which became concerned at the costs involved; but pilot schemes have been floated in several other countries, such as Canada and Scotland, and it is an idea that is likely to keep finding proponents.
27. Woodward, *Lyotard and the Inhuman Condition*, p. 12.
28. See Williams, *Lyotard and the Political*, p. 129.
29. Traverso, *Left-Wing Melancholia*, p. xiv.
30. Ibid., p. xv.
31. Ibid., p. xiv.
32. Vince, 'The Chemical-Physical Type of Humanity', p. 47.
33. See Wilson, 'Lyotard/Monory: Postmodern Romantics', in Lyotard, *The Assassination of Experience by Painting – Monory*, pp. 19–81.
34. See Brooks, 'What's Wrong with the North Pole?', pp. 34–7.

Chapter 7

Aesthetics and Politics

Lyotard wrote extensively on the arts, particularly on painting but on literature and film also. His writings on art alone fill several volumes, much of it in the form of introductions to exhibition catalogues, demonstrating an intense interest in developments in the art world that he kept up to the end of his career.[1] Art comes into the argument in several of his major works as well and it has a special significance for him as an area that he believes has the capacity to escape the demands of grand narrative. Admittedly, not all artists take advantage of this, but Lyotard homes in on those who do to point up the implications for their work and how we should respond to it, as well as the wider implications for his philosophical politics. The link between his aesthetic and political views will be investigated in this chapter, which will also look at his late writings on literature, such as his studies of the work of André Malraux, another very politically committed thinker in French intellectual life, plus his thoughts on film. Lyotard's interest in the arts extended to music as well, but it is art above all that most engages him; as he puts it in *Discourse, Figure*:

> This book takes the side of the eye, of its siting; shadow is its prey. The half-light that, after Plato, the word threw like a gray pall over the sensory, that it consistently thematized as a lesser being, whose side has been very rarely really taken, taken in truth, since it was understood that its side is that of falsity, skepticism, the rhetorician, the painter, the *condottiere*, the libertine, the materialist . . .[2]

Discourse, Figure emphasises the creative element in the arts, regarding this as subverting the power and authority claimed by grand narrative. Creativity is not a rule-bound activity for Lyotard, but something unpredictable that creates new states of affairs and opens up new prospects for others, a situation he will always be keen to lend his support to. The process is like that of postmodern science, encouraging little narratives to keep adding on to the developing discourse, without feeling bound by what has gone on before or being in fear of contradicting received wisdom. Received wisdom has no place in Lyotard's thought; it is there to be contradicted. New phrases can, and must, be introduced to extend the scope of enquiry and generate yet further additions; the system is open to everyone in that respect – although, crucially, no one can own or dominate it. Creativity escapes the grand narrative imperative, therefore, hence the attempt of authoritarian regimes such as Soviet communism to bring it under their control and enforce conformity on it, as the doctrine of socialist reason was formulated to achieve. With its insistence that creative artists follow strict rules laid down by politicians (in the first instance, Stalin, through his cultural commissar A. A. Zhdanov), who saw the arts as a particularly useful form of propaganda for the new communist regime, socialist realism was the antithesis to Lyotard's conception of the arts, which leaned towards the modernist and the openly experimental. Socialist realism, on the other hand, was essentially backward-looking, and very much opposed to modernism, which it regarded as elitist and thus out of touch with the concerns of everyday life. The point of the arts for Lyotard was to challenge the conformist impulse that almost all ideologies contain within them, not to reinforce ideologies. Artists who followed the latter route joined the intellectual class that he was so scathing of when it came to philosophers agreeing to put themselves at the service of political regimes (although allowance has to be made for the fact that to fail to do so in the Soviet Union during Stalinist times was to risk incurring the leader's wrath, as individuals like Dmitri Shostakovich amongst many others were to find out to their cost). Art was not supposed to be harmonisable, nor to follow schemes that tried to pretend the world could be made that way. (The art exhibition Lyotard jointly curated with the design theorist Thierry Chaput in 1985, entitled *Les Immatériaux*, was a practical illustration of unharmonisability, in that it could be negotiated in various ways by its audience, there being no specified 'correct' pathway through in the manner of most such exhibitions – no overall 'master' narrative, in other words. Each member of the audience put together their own unique narrative from the contents on offer.) A large part of art's value for Lyotard was its ability to show how these attempts could only fail; it should never be an advocate for them, never speaking for any overarching idea at all: 'there's no *for*, because there is no finality, and no fulfilment. Merely the prodigious power of presentations'.[3]

It is almost as if the presentation makes its impact on us before the concerns of grand narrative, such as the need to explain and contextualise everything we experience, can kick in to structure them. Artists in his view were natural-born pagans, with the most tenuous of relationships to the dominant ideology and the ruling order – the more tenuous the better, one suspects.

This will not be a detailed exposition of Lyotard's considerable output on the arts, more in the nature of an exploration of what it is he wants from the arts and how he uses them in terms of his political theories, what the arts give him to work with.[4] It is politics that dominates Lyotard's thought and that is the case no less when it comes to aesthetics; indeed, the aesthetic reveals the political to Lyotard:

> 'Aesthetics' has been for the politicist I was (and still am?), not at all an alibi, a comfortable retreat, but the fault and fracture giving access to the subsoil of the political scene, the great vault of a cave on which the overturned or reversed recesses of this scene could be explored . . . For the operations concealed in the production of ideologies can be induced from those of desire exhibited in the production of 'works' of art.[5]

I will be sampling my way through some of his main interests in this area to show how the link between the aesthetic and the political works, and to bring out the political dimension to his writings on art in particular.

Duchamp and Aesthetic Indeterminacy

Marcel Duchamp is an artist who particularly fascinates Lyotard, someone whose art deliberately sets out to defy classification, a trait that Lyotard consistently prizes. A work like *The Bride Stripped Bare by Her Bachelors, Even*, as a case in point, has a very indeterminate character which resists, or at the very least sets up considerable barriers to, critical interpretation – inherently unharmonisable, in other words. (Duchamp's installation work, *His Twine*, for the *First Papers in Surrealism* exhibition in New York in 1942, went so far as to set up physical barriers to the audience's engagement, with the twine strung up between the paintings preventing access to the pieces on show in the room.) Duchamp's ready-mades (the most notorious of which was a urinal, titled *Fountain* and signed as the work of one R. Mutt), challenge the very notion of what it means to be a work of art as well

114

as the viewer's relationship to that, since in Duchamp's provocative description, they feature 'a total absence of good or bad taste'.[6] By deliberate policy on the part of the artist, therefore, neither *Bride, His Twine,* nor the ready-mades fit any standard set of aesthetic criteria by which they could be assessed and contextualised within the history of art, turning them into a form of post-art, or even anti-art. For Lyotard, tellingly, what most characterises Duchamp's art is its 'pointlessness', the result being that from a critical perspective there is 'something uncommentable' about it and that is a condition that neither critics nor the general public will ever be comfortable to find themselves being placed in.[7] For Lyotard, however, that is precisely why art is so important.

Postmodern aesthetics developed a very different set of priorities, with Charles Jencks encouraging creative artists to 'double code' their work by means of a 'radical eclecticism' of styles such that it could simultaneously appeal to both a popular and a specialist audience, thus becoming commentable across the social spectrum.[8] Architecture went in for this with considerable enthusiasm and double coded, radically sometimes very eclectic, buildings are to be found throughout most Western urban centres. It was to be work designed to promote engagement, not deflect it, and it largely succeeded in doing so. Lyotard, however, rejects the need for there to be something to identify with; art should not be so accommodating in his view. It is the lack of a frame of reference that most attracts him when it comes to Duchamp's work, the sense that by its indeterminacy it eludes appropriation by any grand narrative, constituting a powerful example of dissension by its mere existence. It is the kind of work that socialist realists could only loathe as elitist and decadent; pointlessness would be to them an act of open rebellion on the artist's part, deserving harsh punishment for its denial of art's social role. For Lyotard, on the other hand, pointlessness signals something very positive: the limits of the power of grand narrative. Grand narrative does not know what to do with work like Duchamp's; it is left baffled by the experience, so in that rather paradoxical way it is work that also has a social role in the effect it has on its audience, which is being challenged to reconsider its worldview and what it is based on. (Although one observation that should be made is that artists like Duchamp do not reach a mass audience, so the impact of work like this on the public consciousness is unlikely to be all that dramatic. That is always going to be a problem when making claims about modernism, particularly its less celebrated practitioners.)

Modernisms and Postmodernisms

The more that the creative arts can prevent ideological appropriation then the more valuable they are for Lyotard, and this inclines
him towards avant-garde, modernist artists of Duchamp's radical
nature, individuals who are openly challenging social norms and
thus undermining authority. It also puts him at odds with the more
standard version of the postmodern aesthetic put forward by theorists such as Jencks, which actively welcomed appropriation, with
its sense of irony and mix of past and present styles (pastiche being
a characteristic) being enthusiastically received by the advertising
world, bringing it right into the forefront of popular culture. As
Gilbert Adair noted,

> [T]he past (mostly the recent past) has been transformed into a mammoth
> lucky dip. All you have to do, if you are a maker of TV commercials or
> pop promos, a designer of shop windows or record sleeves, the editor of
> *The Face* or *GQ*, an architect, a painter, even a marketing entrepreneur,
> is plunge in and scoop out whatever happens to address your particular
> need.[9]

Adapted that way, postmodernism became a trend and like all trends
it had its moment and then soon came to be seen as passé, generating
a reaction against it in both creative and theoretical circles (although
it has hung on to an extent in architectural practice, where it had first
made its mark). Nicolas Bourriaud, for example, put forward a spir-
ited defence of the modern in artistic practice, arguing that it still had
a critical role to play, coining the term 'altermodern' to indicate how it
could be developed in a post-postmodern context to reflect the positive
characteristics of the modernist approach.[10] Whereas postmodern artists had deliberately rejected experimentalism and the restless search
for originality that had marked out the modernist era, Bourriaud felt
this ought to be continued and that it was shortsighted to dispense
with these objectives altogether. Postmodernism had become rather
facile, a style that was only too easily reproduced and taken over by
the advertising community and the media: an art that held none of the
shock value that modernism was always on the lookout for, double
coding working against that effect. In Lyotard's terms of reference,
that style of postmodern art had been absorbed by the grand narrative
of Western culture and had even willingly cooperated in the process.
Once you became part of popular culture there was no way back.
That kind of collusion was something Lyotard could never accept,

whether it came from artists or philosophers. Both activities ceased to be authentic when they surrendered their power to disrupt and promote dissension. The difference between Lyotard's postmodernism and the popular version of the term comes into sharp focus at such points; anything that serves to support the cause of grand narrative arouses his suspicions, and double coding in the arts, with its appeal to the familiar, certainly could give that impression. Yet, just as it has been observed that modernism can take many forms, we can also say that so does postmodernism; there are modernisms and there are postmodernisms. Lyotard is reacting against modernity rather than modernism, but that is just as much a part of postmodernism as double coding; like post-Marxism, postmodernism is a fairly broad church and can encompass various reactions to both modernity and modernism. Neither Jencks nor Lyotard should be considered to exhaust what postmodernism can mean.

For a useful analogy, it helps to think back to the music scene of the 1920s and 30s, when modernism broke down into various styles that were often contradictory in intention. The twelve-tone system (serialism) devised by Arnold Schoenberg was pushed hard by devotees as the only authentic way to compose in the modern world, given that it involved such a dramatic break with past practice and tonality – and by implication the culture it represented, discredited as this had been by the horrors of the First World War. At the same time Igor Stravinsky became the figurehead of neoclassicism, a style drawing on the forms of the past to produce music largely within the tonal idiom (often reworking actual pieces by composers from previous generations in the 'lucky dip' fashion noted by Adair, as in the Pergolesi-inspired ballet score *Pulcinella*). Neoclassicism has been referred to as 'period modernism', which contextualised it within its own time, even though its models were in the past.[11] The point is that it had to be compared with its contemporaries rather than with those models. Rather like the double coding style of postmodernism, neoclassicism sought to appeal to a wider audience who could identify with its reworking of familiar past styles. Perhaps double coding might be dubbed 'period postmodernism' to differentiate it from the more radical kind of postmodernism favoured by Lyotard and Bourriaud. It is not unreasonable, therefore, emphasising the 'broad church' notion, to use postmodernism as an umbrella term for the shift away from high modernism and modernity that marked out late-twentieth-century aesthetics and critical theory.

Newman: No Allusions

Barnett Newman is another artist that Lyotard is particularly drawn to, finding in his work an unsettling quality which calls to mind the experience of an event:

> Newman's *now* which is no more than *now* is a stranger to consciousness and cannot be constituted by it. Rather, it is what dismantles consciousness, what deposes consciousness, it is what consciousness cannot formulate, and even what consciousness forgets in order to constitute itself.[12]

Like Duchamp, Newman appears to resist interpretation. In his work,

> there are no allusions. So much so that it is a problem for the commentator . . . There is almost nothing to 'consume', or if there is, I do not know what it is. One cannot consume an occurrence, but merely its meaning. The feeling of the instant is instantaneous.[13]

For Lyotard, Newman's paintings make the viewer aware of the fact of the sublime, an inexplicable phenomenon which brings us up against the limits of human power and reason (not just no allusions, but no illusions of a grand narrative kind to be noted either). That is the sort of effect that Lyotard is always seeking from art, fitting in with his rejection of grand narratives and universal theories. Art like Newman's or Duchamp's points up the futility of grand narrative, demonstrating how you can evade its clutches, and so in their oblique way both are helping to undermine the claims of authority; their work just happens, there are no allusions, nothing from which to construct a coherent narrative or assign a specific meaning. Again, nothing could be further away from the aims of socialist realism; on the one hand we have propaganda, on the other pointlessness and indeterminacy, but both are scoring political points nevertheless. Socialist realism represents an attempt to deny the existence of the sublime (or at least the importance of it in human affairs), whereas to Lyotard that is the primary responsibility of the artist, to bring us into an awareness of the sublime, even to shock us into that state. That is one of the criteria he deploys to analyse art; although analysis is probably too strong a word to describe Lyotard's discussion of artworks and criteria too definite a concept for someone who claims to be operating without criteria as a thinker (Dolorès Lyotard has made the interesting suggestion that we should regard his writings on art 'as written *portraits* of the painted work').[14]

It could even be said that Lyotard is an anti-critic in that he does not seek to explain works of art, rather to record the effect they have on him. There is nothing wrong in that of course, and other critics do the same; it would be odd if they did not, but they would not stop there. Almost any other critic would start out with the assumption that there must be something there to 'consume' and, relying on their knowledge of art history, they would undoubtedly find allusions to talk about and influences to note, thereby situating someone like Newman in a historical context; that is the business of art historians, and it can be very illuminating to the general public. It is characteristic of Lyotard, however, to concentrate solely on the work in front of him without reference to the tradition that lies behind it; to acknowledge that would be to predetermine one's response to at least some extent, almost to grant the tradition the status of a grand narrative. Lyotard is open to attack for taking such an approach, which is not of much help to anyone coming at the work of artists like Newman or Duchamp for the first time, and one can often wonder if his evasion of context is overdone: not everyone will be drawn to pointlessness, or allusionlessness (the question of impact raises its head again). Once one is versed in Lyotard's philosophical concerns one can see why he writes about art the way he does and what it is that he wants from artists, but it tells us more about those concerns than about the art in question. The art constitutes evidence for those ideas, to the extent of presenting them to the viewer. It is a very specialised form of criticism that we find in Lyotard, therefore, and it will not be to everyone's taste – certainly not to ideologically motivated commentators, and they still make up the majority of the critical community. It is, however, invaluable to understanding his philosophical objectives and development as a thinker. In art, as elsewhere, Lyotard seeks out the 'here and now' quality, which to him undermines the claims of tradition, and Newman proves an excellent source of this, having produced sculptures entitled *Here I*, *Here II* and *Here III*, as well as a painting entitled *Now*.[15] Newman does his best to evade ideology and theory, and therefore interpretation – precisely what Lyotard feels artists ought to be doing, taking 'the side of the eye'.

Monory: No Story

Lyotard had a long association with the painter and film-maker Jacques Monory, writing several pieces on him which form the basis of the book *The Assassination of Experience by Painting – Monory* and even collaborating with him on some of his film work. Monory was one of the leading figures in the Narrative Figuration movement, which was a reaction against abstract art of the kind that dominated the art scene in the mid-twentieth century. Pop Art was an influence on Narrative Figuration, although it was more critical of the world of popular culture than the leading American pop artists like Andy Warhol were; Monory's work, for example, has many images of violence in it, often drawing on film for inspiration. Despite the 'Narrative' tag, however, Lyotard insists that '[t]here is no story in Monory'; once again, we are being asked to bear witness to 'the prodigious power of presentations' rather than being told what to think or feel or how we might go about interpreting artworks.[16] It is the impact, the instantaneous impact, that is important. The characteristic blue wash over Monory's paintings further distances us from a narrative reading of them in the manner of the figurative tradition; as Lyotard puts it, the colour 'suspends history and so nothing happens in it'.[17] We are back with the instant, the now, a condition that resists interpretation.

Monory's style is for Lyotard intriguingly placed 'between photography and the avant-gardes, or rather at their intersection' and that in-between quality is something that Lyotard will constantly be on the lookout for in discourse of any kind (as we shall see he is with cinema as well).[18] In such a state nothing has been determined yet, meaning that we are outside the framework of grand narrative, in a position where something completely unexpected can happen. Sarah Wilson emphasises this concern of Lyotard, arguing that when it came to Monory's work he 'situated these texts as liminal, on a threshold between the past and a new era'.[19] Lyotard has an abiding interest in the unpresentable, in what cannot be captured or portrayed, in other words what cannot be controlled by grand narrative and thus signals its limitations. That is what he finds in Monory's work, which cannot be pinned down in traditional critical terms because of its liminal quality. We are made aware that there is something that must always escape us, that not everything can be explained – as theories such as Marxism and structuralism would have us believe. We only need to think of the sublime to realise that this is so.

Marxists would feel that they had to place Monory in terms of the class struggle and discuss whether or not his work reinforced or challenged the dominant ideology of capitalism; the notion of anything being able to escape such a debate, and the judgements that inevitably would accompany it as to the artist's political position, would strike them as inexcusable. The social role of art is what matters above all and artists are expected to be in dialogue with the public on those terms; their art has to mean something that the general public can understand, not to leave them puzzled as to what is actually going on in the artwork. Structuralists would find a grammar to Monory's images and relate it to others in the field (Roland Barthes would have had no problem with such an exercise). Culture is eminently explicable to such thinkers, whereas for Lyotard it can never be reduced to the constraints of a universal theory, and any claims that it can be should be treated with the utmost suspicion. All art is political as far as Marxists are concerned and can be interpreted as such. While it has political connotations for Lyotard these are of a very different character than for a Marxist commentator, undermining not just the capitalist grand narrative but grand narratives in general. For Lyotard, art reveals what our politics lacks.

Monory acts as a catalyst for Lyotard's metaphysical speculations, as he notes in the text 'Libidinal Economy of the Dandy':

> This work that follows is situated in libidinal and political economics at the same time as that is where it locates the object of discourse, in this instance the painting of Jacques Monory. This work should be understood as dreamwork, as connection and transformation of the blue canvases into words.[20]

What he is not going to do in this piece is explain what Monory's art means in the traditional manner of the critical theorist or the art historian; instead he wants to bring out a more complicated political process that is at work, one that enables him to explore his own preoccupations: 'to examine how the two set-ups, that of "classical" painting – to which Monory's oeuvre belongs, to an extent that remains to be determined – and that of capital, connect up with each other'.[21] That connection is to be found in the impact of the libidinal on each of them, the concern that runs through Lyotard's attack on Marx in *Libidinal Economy*. A Marxist critic would interpret the painting as the product of a capitalist culture, but to Lyotard that would be a case of the theory imposing a meaning on the art, with the intention of reinforcing the theory's power – exactly what grand narratives are always out to achieve, and Lyotard to challenge. Such politically motivated assessments do not allow for the effects of libidinal desire, which inevitably will serve to undermine them, as the work of artists such as Monory indicates. It is to be treated as dream-work, and Lyotard is to draw on Freud's assertion that 'the dream-work does not think', arguing that '[t]he dream-work is not a language; it is the effect on language of the force exerted by the figural (as image or as form)'.[22] What this means for Lyotard is that we should not try to impose structure on it, particularly any kind of deep structure (Lyotard taking issue here with Jacques Lacan, who had argued that the unconscious was structured like a language).[23]

Lyotard on Literature

Lyotard's modernist inclinations can be seen again in the authors he chooses for study, with Marcel Proust and James Joyce attracting complimentary attention as authors whose writings make us aware that there is 'something which does not allow itself to be made present' in our existence.[24] Whereas modernist creative artists could evince anxiety about this condition, or even a sense of nostalgia for a supposedly lost organicism in our culture, their postmodern counterparts deliberately set out to make us aware of it, while making it clear that it lies completely outside our control and that we can never second-guess what it might do. In the case of Laurence Sterne's *Tristram Shandy*, that means the hero's life is punctuated by a series of accidents and unforeseen events that disrupt any plans he might have. It is as if a malign force is acting against him (a curse shared by his whole family) and he can only observe its adverse impact with a wry melancholy, bemused at his fate: 'What is the life of man! Is it not to shift from side to side? – from sorrow to sorrow? – to button up one cause of vexation! – and unbutton another!'.[25] What such work tells us is that a total picture or full understanding of the world is never possible and that is what Lyotard will seek from authors: literature that undermines itself – and is doing so deliberately. He can find this effect even in some classic authors, such as Cervantes, remarking that, '*Quixote* recounts an epic whose conclusion is doomed to failure from the outset. By the same stroke, Cervantes strips the voice that recounts the epic of its authority over the sense of the story': the same could be said of *Tristram Shandy*, another notably 'quixotic' narrative.[26] Postmodernism becomes a necessary corrective to modernism for Lyotard, therefore, in a pattern that goes on repeating itself: 'A work can become modern only if it is first postmodern. Postmodernism thus understood is not modernism at its end but in the nascent state, and this state is constant'.[27]

(Interestingly enough, Sterne's work has been claimed by both modernists and postmodernists.)[28]

When it comes to André Malraux Lyotard finds several aspects of his writing to admire, despite its traditional form (Malraux is no modernist in the Joycean sense and he is also guilty, as Lyotard sees it anyway, of 'some compositional shortcomings', such as his fondness for the epic, and a self-consciously eloquent style).[29] For a start, Malraux is a staunch opponent of the totalitarianism that flourished during the 1930s and 40s. He is, as Lyotard sums it up, an author who 'distrusts manifestoes and treatises' and is also 'incapable of believing in radiant futures', traits that he will always applaud.[30] Long-range planning is to Lyotard a misplaced activity, almost certain to be overturned by events, which will make the prospect of 'radiant futures' unlikely, little more than wishful thinking in effect, as the two massively destructive world wars in Malraux's lifetime demonstrate only too clearly. Politically, it is best to travel light and the Malraux of the 1930s and 40s can be described as doing that compared to the bulk of his contemporaries – the assorted fascists, communists and nationalists clashing with each other throughout the troubled Europe of the period. Lyotard also notes approvingly that 'there is no trace of anti-Semitism detectable either in the writings or in the conduct of Malraux – rarest of exceptions for his time'.[31] Malraux manages to resist giving into the fatal appeal of becoming an intellectual (in Lyotard's definition of the term anyway), remaining an outsider in a period of intense ideological conflict, Lyotard speaking of his 'revulsion at fascism, Nazism, Francoism, and, later, Stalinism'.[32] Lyotard cultivates just such an outsider persona himself, feeling a sense of revulsion at the many competing 'isms' in the political arena, hence he can identify with Malraux, his various 'shortcomings' notwithstanding. Malraux is not using his fiction to propound a grand narrative, making clear his antipathy to ideological wars by refusing to take sides in them. He does not lecture the reader or offer solutions to those wars either and Lyotard can identify with that too, arguing that 'the novels . . . are more dramatic than they are narrative. Focused on the mise-en-scène of dramatic moments, they show rather than tell'.[33] Choosing to show rather than tell amounts to an anti-aesthetic, leaving it to the readers to make their own interpretation of what is being shown, drawing on their own experience and political concerns. Marxism, on the other hand, is an aesthetic very much committed to telling.

Lyotard on Film

In his early writings on film, Lyotard expresses some reservations about it because it is so ordered and organised a medium, his preference generally being for experimentalism in any art form, for rougher edges and looser structures that do not dictate what the audience's response should be. As with his interests in the fields of literature and art, Lyotard's modernist sensibility comes to the fore with film too, although he was to engage more with mainstream cinema later in his career. In writings like 'Acinema' Lyotard treats film as a fairly conservative medium, concerned to produce a unified artefact. This is very much the case when we think of Hollywood's output, which avoids the controversial as a matter of principle, staying as non-offensive as possible. For the Hollywood studios the point of film is to entertain us, not to shake up our worldview; to do the latter would be to lose a large part of your audience – and your profits too. Lyotard emphasises the highly constructed quality of film-making, where mise-en-scène functions as 'an activity which unifies all the movements' that are to appear on screen, with the director effectively working to a master plan; the film script determines what is to happen almost in the manner of a grand narrative.[34] Any evidence of the unpresentable is simply explained away. It is the predictability of film that Lyotard objects to, therefore, the excessive ordering of its elements towards a sense of unity, so that 'all endings are happy endings, just by being endings'.[35] There is a story in this case, something definite to be consumed. Commercial cinema in general comes off badly from this assessment, with Hollywood again providing the model for others to follow, especially given its all too apparent preference for happy endings that induce a 'feelgood' sensation in the audience (although to be fair, exceptions to the rule have become more common in recent years). Lyotard's alternative suggestion is what he calls 'acinema', an experimental approach that 'would be situated at the two poles of the cinema taken as a writing of movements: thus, extreme immobilization and extreme mobilization'.[36] This would make for a radical departure from what film as a popular medium actually does, its concern to draw the audience into an unfolding narrative that has a sense of reality to it, something they can identify with; pointlessness would hardly fit the bill. Popular film is designed to be seductive, just as grand narratives are, and it is the objective of philosophical politics to point out where and why this is happening, so that we can refuse to be drawn in.

In their study of the concept of 'acinema', Graham Jones and Ashley Woodward point to a 'surprising and dramatic shift of theoretical perspective and style' in Lyotard's work after *Libidinal Economy*, that has an impact on his analysis of film.[37] In his later writing on cinema Lyotard is notably more sympathetic towards the mainstream. He makes some interesting remarks about Francis Ford Coppola's *Apocalypse Now*, for example, finding it intriguing because in one of its most famous scenes, the airborne attack on a Vietnamese village, seduction does not occur:

> The spectator no longer receives from the scene the implicitly given prescriptions to act: *Do this, think that*. He is in a state of loss of obligation . . . The panic is that no narrative can take charge of this chaos of data and suggest an obligation to the addressee. The latter is not seduced.[38]

To Lyotard this scene marks a shift from realism to hyperrealism in the film, and when that happens 'it ceases to seduce', which to him is a mark in its favour.[39] Instead, the viewer 'is made to suffer from an excess of reality' and 'excess of information'.[40] It is as if a social contract has been broken at that point, with viewers being left unable to contextualise what has happened within their ideological system, much in the manner of an event – hence the sense of panic it can induce. Lyotard is drawn towards that unsettling quality in the arts in general: the impact it can have in the 'here and now'. (One might wonder whether far right-wing, Vietnam War-supporting patriots would find the scene seductive, however; the hell of war does have an appeal for such.)

Acinema can come across as an attack on the concept of narrative, certainly on coherent narrative, and experimental cinema often does dispense with that coherence altogether. As an example of anti-narrative cinema, Andy Warhol's *Empire* could be cited. With its eight-hour-long shot of the Empire State Building it would fit Lyotard's criterion of 'extreme immobilisation' and in that respect it could be identified as an example of the pointlessness he praises in Duchamp's work (its ending is quite arbitrary too – it could go on and on). Yet narrative still remains the basis of film as a popular medium (narratological theory providing the basis of most screenwriting in this area),[41] as it does with literary fiction, and audiences expect to be presented with that; the success of Hollywood blockbusters and bestsellers confirms the market demand, and the symbiotic relationship between makers and audiences has to be acknowledged. One does wonder if Lyotard's position is unnecessarily extreme, however, since even the most commercial films can be interpreted in a wide variety of ways, sending out different messages to their audience. We can go back to Roland Barthes and the 'death of the author' notion as a response to Lyotard on this issue, Barthes making it clear that after a text of any kind is released into the world then it belongs to its audience, not its creators: 'the birth of the reader must be at the cost of the death of the Author', as his much-quoted phrase has it.[42] Once individuals engage with a text then it is processed through their own experience, taking it further and further away from its creator's intentions as to what their response should be (and perceptions of a film can change quite markedly over the years, taking it yet further from original intentions as it is affected by cultural change). 'Acinema' does not seem to allow for this in terms of film, effectively writing it off as an artistic medium except for its experimental or underground side. Granted that commercial cinema on the Hollywood model can be very manipulative indeed, the possibility that little narratives can be constructed out of almost any text is not being acknowledged. Whatever they may believe, neither the scriptwriter nor the director can dictate totally the reception of a film (especially over time). At least some of the audience can, and will, be resistant to even the most openly manipulative of the makers' efforts, and no master plan can prevent that, no matter how ordered and organised it might be: the 'prodigious power of presentations' still applies and that does not necessarily always deliver happy endings for every viewer. Film is not as finalising a medium as Lyotard implies in his early work on the form.

Lyotard's early views on commercial cinema can be challenged, therefore, although the political imperative behind these can be understood. He is a consistent opponent of manipulation of our thoughts and emotions, of a knowing seduction of the addressee, which is one of the main methods used by grand narratives to maintain their hold on power (fascism is particularly efficient at this, with its cynically calculating aestheticisation of politics to create spectacles with mass appeal), and film is a medium which goes in for this in a big way, expertly using its myriad of resources to induce the response it wants from its audience. It is all very carefully worked out by the major studios (narratological schemes being consistently deployed), designed to capture a mass audience and dictate how it will respond to its productions. A similar point could be made about television, as well as theatre and opera (Richard Wagner quickly jumps to mind, with his 'total work of art' (*Gesamtwerke*) approach), but film is a more immersive medium than any of these, and it is that aspect of it which Lyotard finds most problematic: film's power to dominate our attention to such a remarkable degree. Fortunately, it is possible to overcome the seduction imperative, not to 'do this' and 'think that' as directed, not to go along with the happy ending, although it does take some serious reflection on the part of the individual to do so. Lyotard's theorising on film points the way towards that, fitting in with his general philosophical concern to subvert grand narrative. The creative arts have that subversive potential, even if artists often fail to take full advantage of it, and thus have considerable symbolic importance for Lyotard.

Lyotard on Television

Lyotard's appearance on the French television programme *Tribune libre* in 1978, entitled 'A Podium without a Podium: Television According to J.-F. Lyotard', is worth a mention here, given its distinctly experimental format and what this says about Lyotard's conception of his role as philosopher in the public eye. Soundtrack and image are out of synchronisation for most of the proceedings and in the accompanying commentary Lyotard refers to himself in the third person. The programme's disjointed quality and lack of coherent narrative line is akin to what Lyotard finds attractive about experimental cinema, as if he were exploring the extremes of the television medium ('atelevision' perhaps?) – and of his audience's patience too, one would think. It is as if he is not taking the project seriously, as one suspects almost any other academic figure in French life would have done, regarding it as a welcome opportunity to make their mark on public debate and thus enhance their reputation. Asked by the programme makers to participate as an 'intellectual' (all but a red rag to a bull in this case), Lyotard does his best to distance himself from such a notion, insisting firmly that he 'refuses to appear before your eyes and ears as an authority, as he is asked to do'.[43] The general tone of his commentary is mocking, Lyotard provocatively asserting at another point that although in his academic role 'he does philosophy. No one has ever been quite sure what that consists of', not the most helpful thing for a professional philosopher to tell his audience.[44] (It would be hard to imagine a British philosopher making a similar statement on television now, given the various government audits that the UK's university system has had imposed on it, with demands for demonstrating the public impact and social significance of one's subject area a very prominent requirement in order to bring in funding; the institution's management most likely would be appalled.) Lyotard is never one to offer platitudes; he will always make his audience work and in that sense he does know what philosophy consists of for him: it is a means to critique the concept of authority in whatever medium he happens to be working in, to bring out its flaws and unwarranted pretensions to power. One does suspect that most audiences would want more than that from the subject, but sceptics down the years have not been prepared to go any further, defiantly taking on the role of the figure within philosophical discourse.

Lyotard's refusal to accept, or play, the role of authority marks a clear distinction with the French tradition of public intellectual as typified so memorably by Jean-Paul Sartre, who would hardly be one to say that he did not know what philosophy consisted of. Existentialism presented itself not just as a philosophy but as a lifestyle, with Sartre, Simone de Beauvoir and Albert Camus as role models for the post-war generation, and its followers really did take it very seriously. Sartre in particular was very much a figure of authority, his work achieving wide recognition internationally, and his journal *Les Temps modernes* delivering trenchant political opinions on the major issues of the day in the post-war period. To Lyotard, however, especially in the aftermath of the *événements*, the public intellectual was a discredited notion and he was not about to use his position and public standing to continue that tradition (as his *Tribune libre* appearance uncompromisingly confirmed). If Sartre had presented himself in the manner of the grand narrative of the public intellectual for his generation, Lyotard was defiantly to make a point of being a little narrative only.

Lyotard on Music

As his tastes in art and literature would lead you to expect, Lyotard also gravitates towards the work of modernists in music, composers such as his compatriot Pierre Boulez, one of the most technically complex and demanding members of the later serial school.[45] Schoenberg had devised serialism (or twelve-tone composition) in the early twentieth century as a way of breaking free from the concept of tonality that had formed the basis of Western music for centuries, and to Lyotard this constituted a direct challenge to the rules and procedures of that particular theory – in effect, the grand narrative of Western musical composition. Schoenberg had considered tonality to be a restrictive system that curbed the composer's imagination, and the atonal serial technique he developed completely abolished it, leading to a revolution that was to create deep divisions in the musical world for generations afterwards: a clear differend, with little in the way of bearing witness going on from either side. Serialism went on to become something of a battleground in the twentieth-century musical world, with supporters and detractors angrily trading accusations and insults with each other. Many composers since have found Schoenberg's serialism just as limiting a method as he considered tonality to be, and there is no denying that it imposes its own strict rules and procedures, replacing one system with another that specifies what the user can and cannot do. It is a highly intellectualised form of composition, with a mathematical sense of order and organisation – not what one would expect Lyotard to champion. He chooses to see it, however, in the larger context of the long-running tradition of Western classical music which had treated tonality as the only natural way to compose and had used it as the foundation of teaching in the academy. Serialism was to change all that, although it has never been a very popular form of composition amongst the general public, making only intermittent appearances in the concert hall (the neoclassical style of such contemporaries of Schoenberg as Stravinsky proved far more acceptable to audiences), and it has few devotees left nowadays, even in the academy, which had in fact embraced it to a significant extent as the twentieth century progressed (leading to the curious situation, as one musicologist has observed, of pupils 'earnestly composing a type of music that they would never dream of actually going to a concert hall to hear'[46] – yet another differend for the individuals in question to wrestle with). It is a style that unsettles listeners who are used to tonality, but not in the positive way that Lyotard wants the arts to do; most listeners tend to avoid it after their first exposure, finding it alien to their understanding of what music should sound like. In the manner of experimental film, it is not entertaining and that is what a majority of people want from the arts in general, rather than ideologically challenging experiences of the type that Lyotard favours. Tonality is still the basis of most of the music composed in the West, particularly when it comes to popular idioms, which had never stopped using that method, so in that sense serialism is now a thing of the past. Lyotard's modernism does date him more than somewhat when it comes to aesthetics.

Boulez was an exponent of what came to be known as 'total serialism' (sometimes 'integral serialism'), which was an even more tightly organised form of composition than Schoenberg used. On the face of it one might have thought Lyotard would be suspicious of work with such an intensive degree of organisation as this, but there were other aspects of Boulez's style that held appeal for him. Boulez was noted for continually revising his scores, as if he was never quite satisfied with the outcome, leaving us with various versions of them (three of *Pli selon pli*, for example). All composers revise at least some of their works over their lifetime as their ideas change and technique develops, but Boulez carries this much further than the norm, constantly tinkering with works already known and performed, leaving various options for performers to pick from. One can see why Lyotard would find this tendency of particular interest since it seems to rule out the possibility of artistic unity, with Boulez continually, as it were, adding 'phrases' to his work in the manner of how Lyotard saw discourse in general as operating. It also problematises the issue of endings, which was a characteristic that Lyotard praised with regard to experimental cinema in comparison to the Hollywood model. Whichever one of the three versions of *Pli selon pli* a conductor chooses for a concert programme, therefore, cannot be considered to be definitive; in fact, the question arises as to whether each revision Boulez makes turns it into a new piece altogether rather than just a modification of an existing one. That is the kind of indeterminacy that Lyotard would appreciate, with Boulez almost working in the manner of a postmodern scientist, refusing to be bound by what had already been established or he already knew. The audience likewise has to keep reassessing their ideas about Boulez, never being allowed to rest on what they know of any of his works. The music critic Alex Ross has remarked that the effect of Boulez's total serialism 'is a music in constant flux', and one imagines that would go down particularly well with Lyotard; constant flux is just what he wants both politics and philosophy to be in, what little narratives are designed to respond to and to promote.[47] (It is worth noting, however, that Boulez, more than something of a firebrand in his younger days, was later to lose his enthusiasm for total serialism, describing it as 'totalitarian' in the demands it placed on the composer.)[48]

With music, as with art, film and literature, it is a case of Lyotard looking for works which exhibit traits that fit with his philosophical concepts and concerns, and Boulez, like Schoenberg before him, provides that (although his 'totalitarian' jibe does raise some interesting issues about serialism, which had seemed to come to regard itself as a new grand narrative out to obliterate tonality). Once again it leads him away from the mainstream and the traditional into areas that force his readers to re-examine their beliefs and the culture they spring from; whatever his topic that will be the effect Lyotard sets out to achieve, his iconoclasm very much in evidence.

Conclusion

From analysing Lyotard's various forays into the creative arts, it becomes clear that what he most prizes is their ability to unsettle the audience, to leave them less comfortable within their society's grand narrative and even moved to question its validity. Postmodern aesthetics on the double coding model does not really provide such an experience, so from Lyotard's perspective it is in effect colluding with the power structures of its society, engaging in seduction on their behalf. He demands much more from artists than that, wanting their work to have the impact of an event, to be disruptive and intensely thought-provoking – as Duchampian pointlessness, or Boulezian total serialism, very notably can be. Mere entertainment is never what he is after (and double coding can provide that, often being very witty in its interplay between past and present forms and themes); it is the political dimension to artworks that draws his attention. There is a social role for art, therefore, although of a very different order from what socialist realism or postmodern aesthetics of the Jencksian kind envisaged it to be. It may not be in a straightforward, polemical way, but thinking art is thinking politics too, and Lyotard will always want to push us towards that state. The aesthetic ought to be an irritant of ideology, not a reinforcement of it, and in that sense it offers a model for politics to follow.

Lyotard is not in the stricter sense an art critic and he could be criticised for imposing his own philosophical and political concerns on the artists to whom he is attracted, using them as a basis to engage in often extended metaphysical speculation. His interest is in works that appear to align with his own views, so there is a specific agenda behind his writings on art and indeed the arts in general (one could not call him a literary, film, or music critic in the standardly understood sense of the terms either). If one were being very critical, one could say that he is interpreting art in much the same way that Marxist critics do: through a set of socio-political ideas that condition his response, even if he does not judge works in such an overt manner as they usually do. Reading Lyotard on art you soon come to know what it is he is looking for, what he is hoping to find, and that will invariably relate back to his critique of grand narratives. Artists like

Duchamp, Newman and Monory are valuable for him because they seem to provide evidence supporting that overall critique, as well as capturing something of the experience of the event, the point where the weakness of grand narratives becomes most obvious. That does suggest a rather narrow perspective on art, and Lyotard could be accused to a certain extent of cherry-picking only what will help to exemplify his theories. That said, however, there is no denying the enthusiasm and seriousness that Lyotard brings to the exercise: art really has enormous importance for him, being a constant source of inspiration. The aesthetic serves as an area where he can test out his ideas and it becomes a lifelong preoccupation that reveals much about his politics. There is a clear political import behind his ongoing project of transforming selected 'canvases into words'.

Notes

1. See Lyotard, *Writings on Contemporary Art and Artists*.
2. Lyotard, *Discourse, Figure*, p. 5.
3. Lyotard, 'Anamnesis of the Visible, or Candour', in *The Lyotard Reader*, pp. 220–39 (p. 239).
4. For a discussion of the implications of Lyotard's work for performance art, see Bamford, *Lyotard and the 'Figural' in Performance, Art and Writing*.
5. Lyotard, *Driftworks*, p. 16.
6. Marcel Duchamp, quoted in *The Art of Assemblage: A Symposium*. The fact that Duchamp is now thought by some to have appropriated the idea for the urinal artwork from the work of another artist, Baroness Elsa von Freytag-Loringhoven, only succeeds in further complicating the issue (see Hustvedt, 'A Woman in the Men's Room').
7. Lyotard, *Duchamp's Trans/Formers*, pp. 69, 12.
8. Jencks, *The Language of Post-Modern Architecture*, p. 13.
9. Adair, *The Postmodernist Always Rings Twice*, p. 17.
10. See Bourriaud, 'Altermodern', in *Altermodern*, pp. 11–24.
11. The term was coined by Lynn Garafola, and is used by Alex Ross in his discussion of the development of neoclassicism in the post-First World War period in Chapter 3 ('Dance of the Earth') of his *The Rest is Noise*, pp. 74–119.
12. Lyotard, 'The Sublime and the Avant-Garde', in *The Inhuman*, pp. 89–107 (p. 90).
13. Lyotard, 'Newman: The Instant', in ibid., pp. 78–88 (p. 80).
14. Dolorès Lyotard, 'Epilogue', in Lyotard, *Writings on Contemporary Art and Artists*, pp. 687–95 (p. 694).
15. See Lyotard, 'The Sublime and the Avant-Garde', p. 89.
16. Lyotard, *The Assassination of Experience by Painting – Monory*, p. 114.

17. Ibid., p. 114.
18. Ibid., p. 88.
19. Wilson, 'Lyotard/Monory', in Lyotard, *The Assassination of Experience*, pp. 19–81 (p. 21).
20. Lyotard, *The Assassination of Experience*, p. 95.
21. Ibid., p. 98.
22. Lyotard, *Discourse, Figure*, p. 267.
23. See Lacan, *The Seminar of Jacques Lacan, Book III*, p. 167.
24. Lyotard, *The Postmodern Condition*, p. 80.
25. Sterne, *The Life and Opinions of Tristram Shandy*, p. 268.
26. Lyotard, *Soundproof Room*, p. 28.
27. Lyotard, *The Postmodern Condition*, p. 79.
28. See, for example, the various contributors to Pierce and de Voogd, *Laurence Sterne in Modernism and Postmodernism*.
29. Lyotard, *Soundproof Room*, p. 10.
30. Ibid., pp. 66, 58.
31. Ibid., p.28.
32. Ibid., p. 16.
33. Ibid., p. 56.
34. Lyotard, 'Acinema', in Jones and Woodward, *Acinemas*, pp. 33–42 (p. 38).
35. Ibid., p. 173.
36. Ibid. p. 177.
37. Jones and Woodward, 'Setting the Scene', in ibid., pp. 3–9 (p. 6). Lyotard's late work, and its relationship to his earlier, is the subject of the various contributions to Bichis and Shields, *Re-Reading Jean-François Lyotard*.
38. Lyotard, 'Two Metamorphoses of the Seductive', pp. 59–61 (p. 59).
39. Ibid., p. 58.
40. Ibid., p. 59.
41. Hollywood likes films which conform to narratological schemes, with appropriate functions assigned to the characters and thematic moves, such as those outlined by Vladimir Propp (heroes and villains in quest narratives, for example); see Propp, *Morphology of the Folktale*.
42. Barthes, 'The Death of the Author', pp. 142–8 (p. 148).
43. Lyotard, 'A Podium Without a Podium: Television According to J.-F. Lyotard', in *Political Writings*, pp. 90–5 (p. 94).
44. Ibid., p. 91.
45. See Lyotard, 'Music and Postmodernity', pp. 37–45.
46. Scott, 'Postmodernism and Music', pp. 182–93 (p. 183).
47. Ross, *The Rest is Noise*, p. 364.
48. Quoted in ibid., p. 399.

Towards a Politics of the Event

I will conclude this study by considering the significance of Lyotard's anti-teleological bias to the contemporary socio-political climate: a climate where the teleological theories of the far right are rapidly gaining momentum to the detriment of the democratic ethos. The overriding concern of his work is to challenge the threat of authoritarianism, and the notion of grand narrative in general, by emphasising the 'unharmonisable' in our existence. Because of that factor no grand narrative can ever exert complete control over its environment, no matter how much its supporters may choose to make that claim – which should be remembered by any who feel themselves in danger of succumbing to the malady of left melancholy. Differends will always get in the way to demonstrate the limitations of even the most carefully worked-out ideological positions or methods of seduction, and to Lyotard that means we have to develop a tolerance for the incommensurable; without that, we are simply deluding ourselves about what is achievable. The Kantian concept of the sublime provides a powerful impetus to Lyotard's thought in this respect, identifying for him the point at which reason reaches its limits, where its explanatory powers can only fail when confronted with such an unknowable phenomenon. The sublime comes into Kant's 'third' critique, the *Critique of Judgment*, and although it would appear to pose a problem for his commitment to reason, it is one that he feels he resolves satisfactorily. As Lyotard describes it: 'The task assigned to the *Critique of Judgment*, as its Introduction makes explicit, is to restore unity to philosophy in the wake of the severe "division" inflicted upon it by the first two *Critiques*' (*Pure Reason* and *Practical Reason*, respectively).[1] Lyotard, however, is not persuaded that the third critique actually manages to achieve this objective (except by some questionable sleight of hand moves to cover up gaps in the argument) and regards the sublime as a disruptive influence to any attempt to put together a unified philosophy: 'The sublime feeling is neither moral universality nor aesthetic universalization, but is, rather, the destruction of one by the other in the violence of their differend. This differend cannot demand, even subjectively, to be communicated to all thought'.[2] As far as Lyotard is concerned the sublime undermines Kant's project and thus, crucially, the notion of a universal theory, compelling us to recognise the incommensurability that the differend is so unequivocally signalling.

Perhaps death could be regarded as the ultimate expression of the sublime, being unrepresentable as an actual state: a frontier where communication unequivocally breaks down, that goes past the point of any possible human experience. Religions traditionally claim to possess a way round this, contextualising death within a universal master plan concocted by a supreme being or beings. Christianity, for example, promises an afterlife in a heaven presided over by a benevolent, omnipotent God, with the Bible being taken as evidence that this state actually does exist, in which case the sublime then becomes something to look forward to, our destiny as human beings (as long as we are careful to live a godly life). Church funeral services traditionally try to make light of the deceased's death, speaking of it as a mere transition to everlasting life, not an end but a beginning. Islam makes similar promises, with its sacred book telling of a paradise awaiting the faithful after death. Unsurprisingly, generations of believers have found the notion of an afterlife a very comforting one, and most religions have some concept of it, with what they consider to be appropriate evidence to back it up (the New Testament account of Christ's Resurrection, for example). Yet for atheists this attempt to explain the inexplicable and thus demystify the sublime has to be seen as illusory. The sublime cannot be breached, nor can it ever be understood in human terms. Depictions of it in the arts and elsewhere tend to fall back on analogy; but as the sublime goes beyond experience they constitute mere guesses, the reality of which can never be confirmed or in any way proved. To Lyotard, all such attempts only succeed in demonstrating the futility of belief in a universal theory. We have to accept both the inexplicable and the incommensurable within human existence, that is all but a precondition of philosophical politics.

The rejection of all claims to possess a universal theory is a key to Lyotard's political thinking in general, and to determine the continuing implications of this, it will be useful to summarise the various concepts he devises over the course of his career to subvert the grand narrative mindset and its stubborn belief in the universal: concepts such as the little narrative, the differend, paganism, figure and the event – the latter being the central concern here.

Living with Events

The event defines the political scene for Lyotard, being unpredictable in its character and the repercussions that follow on from it, 'manifested through its troubling effects, rather than through its presence', as James Williams has summed it up.[3] It lies outside the control of grand narrative and is to be seen as a positive phenomenon on those grounds, constantly creating new states of affairs for little narratives to use to undermine the power of institutional authority. The dissensus that Lyotard considers to be such a critical part of social existence comes to the fore at such points, the figure within institutional authority's discourse that philosophy strives to keep going, or should in his view of the subject; philosophy for him being a matter of 'figuring, and not just conceiving'.[4] The subversive quality to Lyotard's thought becomes very apparent through that phrase: he is not a system-builder, in the way that both Hegel and Marx manifestly are, rather his aim is to destabilise such systems from within philosophical discourse in order to reveal their limitations and unwarranted pretensions. Philosophy ought to be about asking awkward questions that power cannot really process. It is what we would expect of a sceptic: 'Being prepared to receive what thought is not prepared to think' is a duty Lyotard takes very seriously indeed, and that he expects other philosophers, as well as creative artists, to feel equally bound by.[5] That is how systems are to be put under pressure and made to reveal the weaknesses they otherwise try to hide or deny they have. Philosophical politics has a very public role to play in performing this function.

All authority has its limits, therefore, and the event reveals these quite starkly: 'One could call an event the impact, on the system, of floods of energy such that the system does not manage to bind and channel this energy; the event would be the traumatic encounter of energy with the regulating institution'.[6] The point is that the political system will be overwhelmed on occasion, no matter how much it thinks it has protected itself against the unexpected: wars break out, stock markets crash, economies collapse, natural disasters occur (and will probably become ever more frequent as the climate crisis advances) – the list is long in terms of constant threats to the system's survival, its sense of power and importance. Lyotard's conception of the phenomenon differs strikingly from traditional left-wing views of the event as an opportunity to put a revolutionary programme in action, thus substituting one grand narrative for another, the assumption being that afterwards any events that occur can be controlled by the new regime through its supposedly superior ideology. Faith in its innate superiority dies hard in grand narrative believers, and the notion of having to tolerate incommensurabilities does not come into their mindset. What comes through strongly in Lyotard's work overall, on the other hand, is the importance of being as fluid and flexible in one's beliefs as possible, the svelteness notion that he saw as a necessary trait for responding imaginatively to the event, rather than treating it as something to be exploited in the name of yet another grand narrative. To follow the latter route is an act of hubris:

> Wanting to promote oneself as partisan of the event, or to predispose oneself to the event, is still an ethical delusion. It is a property of the bestowal to dispossess us – one cannot predispose oneself to dispossession. The event does not arrive where one expects it; even a state of non-expectancy will be disappointed.[7]

There is an almost anarchistic quality to his thinking on this issue, as there is to post-hegemonic thinking in general, that deserves to be explored to consider what a politics of the event would mean for the left. Traditionally, the left has been just as much in thrall to the grand narrative notion as the right has, both of them refusing to acknowledge the fact of the unharmonisable, assuming that their ideology can provide whatever resolution is required. Any social or political tensions that may be getting in the way are to be blamed on their opponents: loyalty demands that. What the event does, however, is shock us into realising that the unharmonisable exists, that it is essentially inexplicable and that it will catch us unawares every time:

> The event happens as a question mark 'before' happening as a question. It *happens* is rather 'in the first place' *is it happening, is this it, is it possible?* Only 'then' is any mark determined by the questioning: is this or that happening, is it this or something else, is it possible that this or that?[8]

As a definition, this is rather tortuous; but if one were to relate it to an experience which is common to humanity in general, then we might begin to gain a sense of what Lyotard is trying to communicate. That experience is love, which can overtake anyone in that way, causing a disruption in their everyday existence that can readily qualify as an event, being just as inexplicable, unexpected and disorienting. Given Lyotard's periodic ventures into the poetic, I would hope this is not too outrageous an analogy to be making (at the risk of sounding morbid, it could be pointed out that serious illness can have a similarly disorienting effect on the individual).

Lyotard suggests there is an entirely different way of conducting politics, and I would argue that the left has a lot to learn from him on that score – and will have to if it is going to overcome its melancholic tendencies. Events cannot be excised from our existence and will always be there to undermine the pretensions of grand narrative. The notion of total control will always be suspect, an ideological confidence trick that will catch out believers eventually when events hit without warning, as is their nature. 'Thinking politics' means bearing that in mind at all times and not falling prey to the delusions of grand narrative, keeping ideological baggage to a minimum instead in order to be able to respond as creatively as you can to the opportunities that change offers; simply returning to your old ways and beliefs afterwards will not keep the effects of an event at bay. Lyotard's message is that authoritarian and totalitarian imperatives never have as much power as they believe they have and that their weak points will always be vulnerable to pressure from little narratives. Incommensurabilities cannot be hidden away indefinitely, no matter how all-encompassing a scheme the authorities may think they have constructed to overcome them: a theory like Marxism is doomed to fall short eventually. Hence the notion of turning from Marx to Kant that became something of a talking point in later-twentieth-century French philosophy and critical theory, Kant's antinomies (propositions where, despite the fact that they are 'free from contradiction, . . . unfortunately, the assertion of the opposite has, on its side, grounds that are just as valid and necessary')[9] appearing to thinkers like Lyotard to undermine the notion of the dialectic that was subsequently to be developed in the work of Hegel and Marx, in the latter's case underpinning his entire theory of politics, with its vision of societies locked in unremitting class struggle. In 'Judiciousness in Dispute, or Kant after Marx', Lyotard is to argue that the antinomies Kant puts forward are not really contradictory, that in each case they fail to qualify as a thesis and its antithesis. He notes 'the futility of the dogmatic arguments offered on all sides. This futility results from an illusion which causes one regime of presentation to be taken for another'.[10] What we are left with is a differend rather than a dialectical relationship – and that may also be the case with the Marxist dialectic. Going back to Kant reveals a fundamental flaw in dialectical thought, a fairly damning assessment of the Marxist enterprise. The proletariat is not an antithesis to the bourgeoisie, therefore, it is a differend, which demands an entirely different response from us. Carry that line of thought far enough and the whole notion of dialectical materialism begins to crumble. Dialectics comes to seem the most abstract of notions, which simply does not map onto the material world in the way that Marx had claimed.

Collectively, little narrative, the differend, paganism, figure and the event constitute a refusal by Lyotard to be drawn into the grand narrative game: a resolutely anti-grand narrative campaign that he wages throughout his career, continually pointing out where things do not quite add up as the grand narrative authorities claim they do, where every assumption of predetermination can only be false. For all that those authorities may seek to erase difference, that merely succeeds in driving it underground to await the chance of reasserting itself when the opportunity arises – as it inevitably will. Politics is a series of events that act as a perpetual reminder of grand narrative's limitations; evidence that its hegemony is always under threat. Brexit, for example, was just such a reminder. It was an event that the UK's political class was woefully unprepared for and struggled to respond to as it unleashed a series of other events to confuse the issue still further; political life was thrown off course for years as a result. The Trump presidency had a similar impact on the American political scene, with repercussions which soon spread worldwide due to Trump's unconventional, and all too often deliberately confrontational and insulting, approach to international relations (his apparent offer to buy Greenland from Denmark is a notorious case in point). Neither country's grand narrative was designed to cope with such an event, nor to accommodate it within its ideological framework. The disruption that followed in each case was an indictment of the system, undermining its authority in a very public way: 'traumatic encounters' as Lyotard had warned could happen at any time to erode belief in the society's institutions. 'Taking back control' is a meaningless phrase in the face of such events, which alter the political landscape in entirely unpredictable ways that any grand narrative will struggle to encompass within its plans, no matter how much selective 'forgetting' it chooses to indulge in about promises made to the public. One suspects that both Brexit and Trump will haunt their respective countries' political life for quite some time yet and that there will be many more shocks to deal with along the way. It will be less a case of 'be prepared' than 'expect the unexpected' and be sure to discard any 'ethical delusions' you may have been harbouring. Whether the left as currently constituted is up to that is an open question.

Svelte Politics

Svelteness holds the key to coping with a world of events and the traumatic encounters they generate. It is the ability to adapt to each situation as it unfolds, without allowing oneself to be trapped into a set routine or way of thinking: 'it is flexibility, speed, metamorphic capacity (one goes to the ball in the evening, and one wages war the next day at dawn). Svelteness, wakefulness, a Zen and an Italian term'.[11] These were traits that were notably absent in the long drawn-out process that was Brexit, revealing a political class stuck in its own grand narrative and unable to think outside its parameters, hence the series of errors and gross misjudgements they went on to commit. In *Peregrinations*, Lyotard speaks of 'the lightness of thoughts' and that is the basis of svelteness: a recognition that things can change quickly and without warning and that one is never in complete control of how events are developing; you may not even know when you are at a ball in the evening that you will be waging a war the next morning.[12] Events can be responded to, but never directed – except in a very limited sense. Nor can they really be planned for; they almost invariably seem to catch the ruling authorities off guard – the stock market crash that happens seemingly overnight, etc. (the international financial markets constitute a particularly intriguing figure within political discourse at national level, being both autonomous and ruthless in pursuing their own interests, oblivious to whatever the fall-out may be). There are some interesting parallels to note here with the existentialist view of freedom, where it is the mere ability to choose how to respond to situations that defines the concept, even when those situations are beyond our individual control (an all too common state of affairs in most of our lives). To be svelte is to exercise that kind of freedom, where it is the response that is critical: a response based on adaptability and creativity, rather than an unquestioning belief in the infallibility of one's grand narrative, which can only hamper you. Svelteness and lightness would be what would characterise a Lyotardean politics of the event, rather than the clumsy reactions that are usually forthcoming from the traditional political class. A svelte nation state is hard to envisage, as far as the current model of politics is concerned anyway. Brexit has to be regarded as a case study in unsvelteness, damning evidence of a whole series of ethical delusions, to which true believers are hanging on grimly.

It is easier to say what svelteness and lightness are not, however, than what they are – or should be (as we have been finding out repeatedly through this study, Lyotard's concepts tend towards the loose when it comes to definition). One answer might be that they are the characteristics that drive little narratives, which have clearly defined objectives in terms of standing up to the power of grand narratives, but are ready, in fact consider themselves to be obliged, to dissolve the moment those objectives have been achieved. Like clouds, little narratives have no long-term fixed identity, but can dissipate or change shape as circumstances dictate. They are designed to be transitory, and their effectiveness is very much tied up with their ability to emerge quickly, carrying as little ideological baggage as possible and able to act pragmatically; the longer they last then the more likely it is that such baggage begins to accumulate – to detrimental effect. As we have seen, however, there is no reason to assume that they have to be left-wing in character; right-wing little narratives could follow much the same pattern, and that hardly chimes with Lyotard's political outlook. Right-wing extremism can be svelte too, but in all the wrong ways: devious and cunning in its use of post-truth and fake news, for example, which can very effectively undermine the whole democratic system – including those on the left opposing the hegemony of the ruling class. It has to be recognised that dissension can be fomented from the right just as much as from the left. The Tea Party provides a warning in this respect of how the little narrative principle can be abused, and what this can lead to; Nigel Farage's Brexit Party is yet another example of this in action (as was UKIP before it), indicating that it is a longer-term problem for the left to ponder. There has to be a pagan element present in little narrative in order to satisfy Lyotard's vision of its role, and neither the Tea Party nor the Brexit Party can lay claim to that – nor would they want to; their ambitions are far grander and more sinister (they are prime examples of movements where, as Alison Dagnes has neatly put it, the followers are 'Super Mad at Everything All the Time', where 'everything' stands for all those who do not think exactly as they do).[13]

Pagan Politics

Ultimately, Lyotard wants us to approach politics in the spirit of paganism, which for him means emphasising the importance of opinion over ideological beliefs and recognising that has to be the basis of public debate. In a pagan society,

> one will have to judge . . . by opinion alone, that is, without criteria. And here I get back to Aristotle. We are always within opinion, and

there is no possible discourse of truth on the situation. And there is no such discourse because one is caught up in a story, and one cannot get out of this story to take up a metalinguistic position from which the whole could be dominated. We are always immanent to stories in the making, even when we are the ones telling the story to the other.[14]

This passage is worth dwelling on for a bit, in order to tease out its implications for current-day political practice. Opinion is certainly rife in contemporary political debate, but it is all too often delivered as if it were received truth derived from a grand narrative, the legitimating power of which is just assumed by believers to be self-evident – as well as exclusive, a case of either you are on our side or you are just plain wrong. There has always been an element of this in politics, but of late it has become more pronounced than it has been for some time. The far right in particular harbour no doubts about the validity of their beliefs and their superiority over all others, and the far left are just as capable of such a blinkered attitude – classical Marxists, for example, treat Marx's science of society in precisely that way, the answer to all possible social and political problems. Opinion turns into ideology when that happens, and the possibility – not to mention the desirability – of compromise goes off the agenda. Theocracy operates in a similar fashion, as can be seen from Islamic fundamentalism (with historical precedents in other monotheisms). For Lyotardean paganism, however, it is all just opinion, and opinions are subject to the manner in which the (political) story unfolds, constantly having to be reconsidered against events rather than a universal theory that can always be relied upon. We can never escape immanence; we are always situated within a developing narrative that we must keep adjusting to. As a player we can have no access to a 'unitary theory' nor 'unitary horizon' that would give us an advantage over others. The more that all sides could agree on that primacy of opinion, then the healthier our political life most likely would be. Differends could then be negotiated in a spirit of goodwill that is in notably short supply at present (Brexit is always worth a mention at such junctures, with its litany of insults, pathetically self-important posturing and even death threats from the more ardent of the Brexiteers – one of the blunter ways of trying to close down a differend that is annoying you).

In jettisoning criteria pagan politics steers clear of ideology, and that is what Lyotard believes philosophical politics should always be doing, thinking to the moment instead of relying on authority and its claim to possess a metalinguistic position – a position that sceptics have been denying the existence of throughout philosophical history, right up to the postmodernist and poststructuralist movements of our own day. As far as sceptics are concerned, behind any metalinguistic assumption lies an infinite regress. A parliamentary system based on the little narrative principle, as discussed in Chapter 1, would adopt the practice of thinking to the moment as its house style, to be backed up by a pagan style of justice system with pragmatism well to the fore and criteria tailored to fit each situation.

Reassessing the Event

There are aspects of Lyotard's conception of the event, however, that can make us wonder whether it is even more problematic in political terms than he feels it is. Events, after all, can be traumatic in ways that even the most svelte of pagans could struggle to negotiate to their advantage. Politics can be changed for the worse by a fascist coup, or a military coup, both of which have been common enough occurrences in recent history (South America has been particularly bedevilled by the latter, to the point where it has almost become routine, but Europe has had its share too). The Spanish Civil War was an event that led to decades of dictatorship that benefited the right, leaving the left in a state of disarray. The Russian Revolution also resulted in decades of totalitarian rule, despite a start that promised an altogether more egalitarian lifestyle for the country's population, and its effects linger on in a country which is only notionally democratic in the Western sense, being closer to an oligarchy with minimal public accountability. It is not always a positive development that the system is overwhelmed; it might, in fact, be something we should dread happening rather than welcome on the principle that it creates difficulties for the grand narrative we might be struggling under. In Lyotard's view it should give us a sense of perspective as to how limited our powers are, how our efforts can be undermined by events outside our control, and although he considers that to be a positive outcome, it could just as easily induce feelings of pessimism or helplessness in those caught up in the aftermath – especially if they are a prelude to a turn for the worse (events having their own momentum). Lyotard tends to emphasise the opportunities that events present, but these may not always be apparent – as in the case of a right-wing coup, which can unleash some of the worst aspects of human nature, aspects that can be very hard to eradicate from public life afterwards. We cannot prevent events from occurring, but whether they provide a good basis for a politics is a more contentious question, since they cannot really be planned for; before we know it they are in flow and we are being carried along by them whether we like it or not. Human beings do seem to have an inbuilt need to plan, in the political realm as elsewhere, and waiting around for a favourable event would clash badly with that. Events can destabilise little narratives just as much as they can grand, therefore, and the little narratives that survive them may not be ones that the left would want or can deal with all that well (Tea Party, Brexit Party); they may just intensify existing differends, making political life even more antagonistic and toxic. Perhaps we should be very careful what we wish for when it comes to events: they can prove to be setbacks as well as opportunities. There is a bleaker side to Lyotard's thought that we have to come to terms with in that respect, where it is human weakness rather than ingenuity that registers most profoundly – as well as more than a bit depressingly.

Little narrative could be seen as operating within political discourse in the manner of a figure, which raises several possibilities as to how that might work out ideologically. In this context it is worth speculating about whether the concept of the 'deep state' fits the description of either figure or little narrative. The notion of the deep state has been raised to suggest that there could be a potential check to the Trump presidency from outside the formal political system, made up of those in positions of power and influence nationally (institutions, the judiciary, the media, the business community, etc.). Although they have no popular mandate to act, they could have enough power to do so should they choose to use it behind the scenes were Trump to behave, as they would see it, unconstitutionally or particularly rashly in foreign affairs. Rich individuals who finance political parties have precisely that kind of influence (as do owners of the major media) and have wielded it for quite some time now, national politics having become an extremely expensive business to engage in, requiring considerable resource to run campaigns – at which point enter large-scale donors expecting favours in return. Arguments have raged about whether taking action against Trump would count as thwarting the democratic will of the people, and although that is a questionable notion at the best of times one can see a logic to it here. Similar speculation has been voiced about whether Brexit could be affected by a British deep state acting against parliamentary, or government executive, decisions. The deep state is a shadowy concept, and its actual nature, and objectives, would be very difficult indeed to determine. It does, however, seem to have something of the character of the figural within a nation's discourse and it could make its presence felt as a little narrative with a specific goal: to check Trump or Brexit, as cases in point.

Like the Tea Party, however, the deep state could just as easily be a right-wing as a left-wing phenomenon – as in the military or fascist coup possibility raised earlier – and it is hard to see it as a development that Lyotard would want to support; in his terms of reference it would be a gross abuse of authority. Once again it would appear to bring out the negative potential within the little narrative concept, how it could have an anti-democratic effect on political discourse – although how that prospect strikes you would very much depend on your attitude towards liberal democracy as it is currently understood and practised. Democracy, like modernism and postmodernism, can take many forms and be understood in various – not always compatible – ways. Accepting the idea of the figural means that we also have to accept that it could have negative consequences for those of a left or libertarian outlook (a group I would include myself in). It could also generate conspiracy theories, which are never a good idea within a democracy, since they can induce a sense of fatalism and nihilism within the political process, suggesting that the general public is at the mercy of those assumed to be behind the conspiracy: left melancholia can easily set in at such points. The libidinal need not always work out in a positive way either; it can lead anyone into situations which could be exploitative of others – as feminist thinkers above all would want to remind us. Hidden forces that break through into our interactions with others can turn out to be very problematic (as Freud's researches record) and the figural's mystical quality means it could be viewed that way, as something to be apprehensive of in its ability to undermine any plans we might make. Perhaps we could think of figure as something like the 'ghost within the machine': a permanent reminder of the limits to our power and of reason's remit. It is the unexpected that can throw any one of us, and any society, off track at any given moment, and that ought to be a sobering thought. Lyotard certainly wants us to be involved politically and not to let ourselves be cowed and directed by those in power, but his philosophy is also concerned to give us a sense of proportion about what human effort alone realistically can achieve. None of us is immune to the effect of the figural and it can manifest itself in any number of complex ways (perhaps crime could be seen as yet another example of the figural, being something that works against the public interest but that always breaks through in even the most rationally ordered and politically egalitarian of societies?).

Lyotard as a Work of Art

Lyotard maintains a strong political bias throughout his work and suggests many ways that we could conduct ourselves to make a significant impact on our own political scene; it can never amount to control of it, but not to play the game at all is to leave the field open to the grand narrative authorities and assorted extremists – of either side of the political divide. As I indicated at the outset of this study, however, Lyotard is not in the stricter sense of the phrase a political theorist; rather he is someone who is inherently suspicious of political theory in general, firmly committed, as he insists, to figuring and not conceiving. Much of his work is concerned with demonstrating the pointlessness of political theory in general. There is no fully worked-out method for engaging in the political arena in his oeuvre, nothing to resemble a Marxist programme for implementing radical cultural change (as Fredric Jameson complains in his otherwise sympathetic introduction to *The Postmodern Condition*):[15] philosophical politics has no such grand designs, its objectives lie elsewhere. To 'alternate between harassing the state and harassing capital' in the freewheeling style described in 'Lessons for Paganism' is not the kind of approach that Jameson has in mind; it sounds more like the action of a dilettante or even an anarchist, types that Marxists in particular deplore. Marxists could certainly agree about the importance of harassing both the state and capital, but would also want to know how it was to be done, and that is never Lyotard's strong point. It is a fair criticism to say that he tends to deal in generalities when it comes to political organisation and action, although it also has to be noted that this is a deliberate, and I would say entirely defensible, part of his philosophical method. Lyotard is adamant that no theory can deliver a utopian existence; instead, we have to keep committing ourselves to tactical struggles within the various discourses that go to make up a society, discourses that no one can ever hope to master completely or direct to their own ends indefinitely. It is the antithesis to what ideologues of all persuasions, with their grandiose schemes, believe. Hence what Keith Crome has referred to as Lyotard's 'deliberate and consistent refusal to offer to his readers the comforts of conceptual, substantive or even stylistic consistency'.[16]

It makes sense to treat Lyotard, therefore, in the fashion that he urges us to do with Marx, as a work of art; to raid him for ideas and inspiration rather than feeling bound to interpret him, and then apply his ideas, in a literal fashion. The notion of approaching Lyotard as Althusser recommended we should be doing with Marx, painstakingly reading his work line by line, over and over again, to grasp its overall message, would not be particularly productive, since Lyotard, the arch-critic of the grand narrative, had no intention of replicating that idea in his own writings. He never sets out to be an ideologue. We can identify a series of tactical positions to be adopted against the overbearing power of grand narratives, such as the little narrative, svelteness, or paganism, but no overall competing system; that is just not Lyotard's way and he studiously avoids allowing it to happen. Graham Jones and Ashley Woodward capture the chameleonic quality of Lyotard's thought very neatly when they refer to him as someone who 'wrote like a thinker "on the run", his views rapidly changing'.[17] Lyotard is, after all, the champion of the unharmonisable, always intent on showing us where systems fail, where paradoxes arise, where ideology's gaps lie, where differends occur and why they must be respected, why encouraging dissension is in any society's best interests. His way of dealing with such situations is to be as pragmatic as possible, to judge and make decisions according to the circumstances obtaining rather than to rely on universal theories with their set modes of practice; to form opinions but not to feel bound by them indefinitely, since they can only ever be contingent. Lyotard's theorising is a response to what is happening in the here and now, where events are playing out. Past practice does not really come into it to any great extent; svelteness cannot permit it. It is always worth emphasising that Lyotard is not tied to any particular programme, although there are, as I have been arguing throughout this study, recurrent concerns (as well as tactical moves) that span his entire career, collectively constituting what Graham Jones has referred to as 'an often neglected continuity throughout . . . Lyotard's work overall'.[18] It is a continuity of concern, however, rather than one of theory. He takes a similar approach to artistic creation too, which he values for its 'here and now' quality, its ability to disrupt established worldviews and to push thought into new territory where responses will not be conditioned by traditional theoretical models: Marcel Duchamp's 'pointlessness' provides an object lesson in how to go about this. For Lyotard philosophy ought to be more like art, something like a blank canvas on which we work out our ideas, relying far more on the eye than rational thought in our responses; criteria can develop as we go along, depending on what is occurring in the here and now.

There are echoes in Lyotard's commitment to dissension of Gilles Deleuze and Félix Guattari's positing of schizophrenia as a way of refusing to be drawn into the grand narrative system of a capitalist society, of not playing the game expected of one and thus disrupting the social order. That order is designed to deal only with standard kinds of behaviour, with conformity to the social norms, not with individuals determined to harass both the state and capital on a permanent basis and feeling no sense of loyalty at all to the system.[19] Schizophrenia would constitute a particularly powerful form of dissension, running directly counter to what is expected of us as social beings – predictability of character and action. To model oneself on the schizophrenic temperament for political effect would succeed in creating events, and that is something the authorities can only struggle with, since they throw any planning they have devised into a state of disorder. Schizophrenia comprehensively confounds standard socio-political discourse.

There are echoes too in paganism of the concept of nomadism in Deleuze and Guattari, with the aim in both cases being to avoid being pinned down by the demands of rigid belief systems with their set modes of conduct and insistence on conformity. The point about nomads is that they do not have a settled mode of existence; flexibility is built into their lifestyle, which is made up as they go along, depending on the circumstances they find themselves in at any given moment. It is a rather romantic view of traditional nomadic life, it has to be admitted, but what Deleuze and Guattari are out to capture is the sense of freedom from central control that the concept evokes:

> [E]ven though the nomadic trajectory may follow trails or customary routes, it does not fulfill the function of the sedentary road, which is to *parcel out a closed space to people*, assigning each person a share and regulating the communication between shares. The nomadic trajectory does the opposite: *it distributes people (or animals) in an open space*, one that is indefinite and noncommunicating . . .[20]

Nomads are effectively 'deterritorialized', as Deleuze and Guattari put it, rootless and unattached in terms of the state and its social norms, which are seen in purely negative terms.[21] Nomads do not really belong to the system and, as with pagans, they can always go elsewhere if they wish to escape restrictions; they have no stake in any particular political entity, being content to exist on its margins, in it but not of it. The breakdown of belief in ideologies such as Marxism in the period following the *événements* registers only too plainly in this move towards contingency and nonconformity when it comes to one's socio-political commitments. It is very much a *post*-Marxist moment that we are witnessing at this point in French intellectual life; classical Marxism has nothing to offer the *soixante-huitards* in the new political situation that has come about, hence the ever more desperate search to find ways of circumventing it. Schizophrenia and nomadism constitute potential antidotes to left melancholia.

It is the tactical quality to Lyotard's thought, therefore, its lightness of touch with regard to rules and regulations (never more than provisional in his view and certainly never to be taken as binding or in any sense authoritative), plus its openness to events and unpredictability, where I would argue his value lies for the contemporary political world, where the grand narratives of the far right are trying to impose their ideology on the general public with what can only be called a notable heaviness of touch. Lyotard offers us a guide to resistance against such schemes, not a replacement as such: an alternative form of social existence is implied in his work but never codified, because '[t]he delusion that we are able to program our life is part of an ancient fidelity to something like a destiny or destination'.[22] That is a recurrent theme in Lyotard's work. Paganism remains the most flexible of systems, featuring lots of room for manoeuvre, intellectually speaking – room to drift, one might say. That is a critical trait in negotiating the events of an unharmonisable political realm, where neither destiny nor prescribed destination have any role to play, no matter what our ruling class may tell us. Any effort you might make in that direction will be largely wasted; the world is just not set up to allow such unrestricted freedom of action, as events will soon make you realise. You can add phrases to the political conversation, but not dictate what they achieve or the response they draw; you can, however, keep on adding more phrases as the debate unfolds (as can, to lend a notably more sombre note to the proceedings, the far right in general as well as the burgeoning ranks of internet trolls who have come to exercise such an adverse effect on public discourse in recent years).

Dissension and Invention

It is worth considering Lyotard's commitment to dissension in more detail, just in case its implications are not necessarily always as positive as he seems to believe they will be. His argument is that 'invention is always born of dissension' and on the face of it that seems a socially very useful outcome, a way of extending humanity's knowledge and ability to use it for the public good. One problem, however, is that dissension is never very clearly defined in Lyotard's oeuvre (a recurrent problem with his concepts in general). When he uses it in the context of scientific enquiry, as in his concept of 'postmodern science' outlined in *The Postmodern Condition*, then one can see what he is getting at. Dissension here means disagreement with particular theories, methods and hypotheses, which generates the creation of alternative ones by dissenters to the current scientific paradigm; these can then be tested to decide which is the more valid and each newly validated theory pushes enquiry in the field further on in a self-perpetuating process. Gaps in knowledge are filled in and anomalies resolved, without ever exhausting the possibilities of further research: new gaps and anomalies are soon revealed and asking to be explored in their turn. Science thrives in such a dynamic environment, which would seem actively to promote the emergence of little narratives and where grand narratives are accepted as having only a contingent status. Dissension acts as a spur to creativeness in that context. Applied to the political realm, however, the concept looks more dubious. The aftermath of wars tends to spur invention, since the standard socio-political infrastructure has often collapsed – particularly on the losing side, as in Germany's case after both the First and Second World Wars. Revolutions can have much the same effect, as the Soviet Revolution of 1917 indicated (and the French one memorably before that); indeed political crises of almost any description can. Whether this is the way most people would want to live for any length of time is another matter; just how much social breakdown could be considered acceptable in the name of invention, one wonders (countries where civil wars drag on for years are invariably desperate places to live, as Syria currently demonstrates). Brexit certainly involved a great deal of dissension, but that hardly seems like an event worth encouraging either – one that could easily merit the description of unharmonisable, making us wonder if that is such a desirable condition to aim for. It is one thing to be unclubbable, another to be almost professionally contrary.

We might at this point refer to the notion of the 'edge of chaos' in complexity theory, where it is argued that systems are at their most inventive when in that heightened state of almost, but not quite, collapsing into chaos and disorder; that is, when they are having to extend themselves to the very utmost of their inventive abilities, using the 'exquisite control' the position offers, just to remain viable entities.[23] How that state can be maintained and invention kept on being effective in just saving the day is a more complicated matter, however; societies do collapse into chaos on occasion, as the frequent incidence of wars and revolutions throughout history would certainly tell us. When that occurs, then unharmonisability has clearly gone too far, and the reaction can just as easily be fatalism on the population's part as invention (and it should be noted that invention is not necessarily always positive in the effect it has on society either, as thinkers like Carl Benedikt Frey have pointed out). Understandable though such reactions are, they do not help to generate meaningful debate to challenge the system. Opting out in this way just tends to leave the field open to ideological extremists – and there is no lack of those around, ready to pounce on such opportunities.

It could be argued that differends generate a great deal of dissension too, especially when the stronger of the two opposing parties suppresses the other, paying no heed at all to its concerns. When this happens invention may well be the response from the weaker side, in the sense of being forced into finding new ways to keep their cause alive and preserve their socio-political identity (as with colonised nations, or persecuted ethnic minorities, for example). But Lyotard is arguing against allowing such situations to develop; he wants differends to be resolved in a manner that does not involve such oppression. It has to be assumed that some degree of compromise would come into resolving any differend to the satisfaction of both sides in such instances, however, and that sits uneasily with Lyotard's desire to keep promoting dissension. 'Bearing witness' to the differend is another instruction from Lyotard that is never very thoroughly explained, although it implies a solution on the lines of his archipelago concept, where each side has its own territory in which its own belief system holds sway and other parties respectfully keep their distance. Apply that to something like the Israel-Palestine situation and you would come up with the 'dual state' idea, where both sides would co-exist in the same territory, free, in Lyotard's terms of reference, to implement their own language game without fear of any interference from the other. Yet as the Israel-Palestine situation indicates, it is one thing to put forward such an idea, which has been around for some time now in diplomatic circles, quite another to put it into operation. Instead, we seem stuck in a classic differend of the traditional variety in this instance, where the stronger side refuses to cede any of its power in favour of its weaker opponent, claiming there can be only one territory with one ruling authority in charge. The notion of sovereignty tends to be interpreted in such an uncompromising way and has been a source of many bitterly contested differends throughout Western history in particular. Even intense diplomatic activity over several decades has failed to stop this process, which has gradually extended to the Israeli practice of walling the Palestinians into ghettoised areas, thus only too graphically demonstrating the former's physical superiority. Negotiating a differend from such an intrinsically unharmonisable position, more reminiscent of apartheid than a dual state, is anything but straightforward. Take away shared goodwill and differends simply strengthen to the point where even pragmatism has little chance of bridging the divide. What one side would consider an advantage, the other would a disadvantage, with little chance of any agreement as to what would constitute a fuzzy weighted average acceptable to both sides – and fuzziness is anathema to dogmatic defenders of traditional sovereignty (as Brexit also revealed). The weaker side cannot be expected to bear witness to the differend under such circumstances, when their oppressors manifestly are not doing so; and it is a sad fact that differends have a habit of working out in such an intrinsically unfair manner, where the operative criterion seems to be that might makes right. Bearing witness in Lyotard's sense of the term is not always an available option, therefore; neither is it entirely clear how it can be made to be so in the face of implacable opposition, which can only generate an unhelpful form of dissension based on resentment.

Another version of the dual state notion can be found in the model that was announced when Hong Kong was returned to Chinese control, after the treaty leasing it to the UK reached its term in 1997. Hong Kong had developed in a very different way from China, a Western-style capitalist entity with a vibrant financial sector, as opposed to a tightly controlled, highly centralised communist state; but the communist rulers promised to respect its identity, stating that China was now to be considered one country with two systems (when Macau later reverted to Chinese control from Portugal in 1999, that lease treaty also having lapsed, some humorous remarks were made about China now being one country with three systems, although Hong Kong, with its far more developed economy and well-established international connections, was always going to be the main focus of Chinese interest). The idea was that Hong Kong could continue much as before, while accepting that political power ultimately lay with the

152

central government in Beijing; in effect, it was to be treated as semi-autonomous, a 'special administrative region' as it came to be called. This particular solution has not worked out very well, however, and Hong Kong is in open revolt against Chinese government policy as I write. Relations have in fact been somewhat strained almost from the beginning of the reunion, with periodic protests against central government meddling in the territory's affairs the rule. Having apparently agreed to bear witness to the differences prevailing, the Chinese state has instead reverted to the well-worn differend solution of the stronger party pulling rank and bullying the weaker (with the threat of physical force always lurking in the background, in this case from the formidable People's Liberation Army (PLA)).

Yet in principle the notion of two, or even more, parallel systems within one polity is not impossible to envisage. Britain could well be divided into Leave and Remain systems as a result of Brexit, the former out of the EU, the latter in. It would be federalism taken to another level and given that leaving Europe has sparked a surge in calls for Scottish independence it could happen after a fashion, the Scottish government having made clear its desire to join the EU in the event of independence (it may well have happened by the time this book comes out, but even if it has not, it will remain at the forefront of Scottish political discourse as a possible move that could be triggered at any point if relations with England were to become fraught enough). Northern Ireland poses yet another intriguing situation, with calls for a united Ireland becoming more widespread since the Brexit referendum, which, as in Scotland, showed a definite majority for Remain there too. The 'Irish backstop' idea, which was suggested as a way of avoiding a hard border between Northern Ireland and the Republic, would have led to a two-system model if it was ever implemented, with Northern Ireland still being in the EU when mainland UK was not. It was repeatedly rejected by the Westminster parliament, but the fact that it was even put forward at all indicates that the need for creative solutions out of political impasses has been recognised by at least some of the political class (and solutions that are as pragmatic as they are creative too). Such inventiveness is only too welcome in an era where dogmatism is making it so difficult to find space for bearing witness.

Picking up on Ioan Davies' criticism that Lyotard's concept of the Jews was on the abstract side, perhaps the same point can be made about the concept of bearing witness. Although it sounds like a principled and decisive stand to take, there is a vagueness about it in terms of the actions and procedures it would require to make a truly meaningful impact in the political domain. We know when it has not taken place, as in the case of Martin Heidegger and Nazism, but in more general terms it is unclear exactly what we are being asked to do; never allowing ourselves to forget acts of injustice would be a start, but no more than that. Taking a more positive line, however, it represents an invitation to us to develop the notion politically; at the very least it is a very suggestive concept ethically, requiring us not just to acknowledge differends but to feel under an obligation to seek out ways of resolving them that do not involve an injustice being done to either side in the process. Lyotard is urging us not to become part of the majority that generally chooses the status quo in such instances; in effect, this amounts to a tacit refusal to face up to the differend, and it works to the benefit of the authorities.

'How to Judge Jean-François Lyotard?'

Derrida's question 'How to Judge Jean-François Lyotard?' lies behind any study of Lyotard, given the immense importance of the concept of judgement in his work; it is an issue that keeps arising in some form no matter what he is writing about, as one would expect of a relativist with such a strong commitment to politics. In reaching any conclusion about it, perhaps we have to go back again to the notion of treating Lyotard as a work of art, there to be raided for ideas and tactics on how to resist and subvert the oppressive schemes of established authority, rather than expecting a fully worked-out, watertight political theory to emerge from such a substantial body of writings covering such a wide diversity of topics: Lyotard's range, with what might be called its 'radical eclecticism' of interests, is never less than impressive. Even if there is an abstract, often vague sense about his concepts and how they should be applied (as other commentators have observed),[24] he very capably identifies the wrongs that need to be addressed, wrongs that are endemic to the ideological systems that seek to exert control over our politics. His conviction in doing so remains admirably constant and focused. Thinking politics without a grand narrative is never going to be less than a complex process, however, involving many detours, shifts of emphasis and, on occasion, paradoxes, and we need to bear that in mind when assessing Lyotard. Grand narrative is always going to be the more comfortable position for any political thinker to adopt (even left populism has an implicit belief in this, with distant echoes of Marxism behind it), in that it provides set methods and answers to any problem that arises, its teleological bias being quite blatant. The problem is that those answers are mostly illusory, and while it would be understandable if a thinker like Lyotard were to fall into nihilism, or a debilitating left melancholia, on realising this was the case, given the level of public support that grand narrative is still capable of drawing, he bravely battles on trying to construct pragmatic ways out of this quandary (identifying a dialogue with nihilism in Lyotard, Ashley Woodward argues that it is crucial to an understanding of his later thought, that 'he develops a theory of nihilism that complements a theory of the postmodern condition': a non-defeatist nihilism, in other words).[25] To accuse him of 'latent amorality' is to miss this critical aspect of his philosophical career. I would describe him instead as one of the most principled thinkers of his generation. Even in *Libidinal Economy*, his self-defined 'evil' book, he is striving to bring grand narrative to judgement, albeit with his frustration at the pretensions of Marxist theory and practice on full, almost embarrassing, display. If the book can admittedly sound nihilistic in tone much of the time, with its scathing assessments of Marxism and intellectuals as a class, nevertheless it still has the underlying motivation that drives Lyotard's philosophical politics – the destabilisation of the grand narrative concept. Indeed, it is arguably never more apparent than it is there, delivered with such extreme emotional intensity, as if he could hardly contain his anger at having to point out Marxism's (to him glaringly obvious) deficiencies. Thinking politics cannot stop, not with the pretensions of the grand narrative culture continuing to have such a powerful effect on the body politic and forming the basis of our system of justice. Nihilism becomes a way of dismissing the claims of grand narrative – and with inciting us as readers to do the same thing. Samuel Beckett might be seen as a kindred spirit here, in that his work has drawn accusations of nihilism as well; but there is a positive side to it in his characters' determination to keep going despite the troubles, above all the pervasive sense of pointlessness, of their lives.[26] Nihilism can be considered a form of cultural critique for both writers, and 'Fail again. Fail better' an injunction just as applicable to Lyotard as to Beckett; whatever you do, you do not give up, no matter how hopeless the situation may appear to be, or how 'rebellious' the language and politics.[27]

That is probably the key message to be taken from Lyotard's work overall: that we should never cease thinking politics beyond what our grand narratives tell us we should be thinking, never simply conforming to the status quo as being too powerful to challenge. In one of his more poetic moments, Lyotard describes this state of mind as a case of bearing 'witness to what really matters: the childhood of an encounter, the welcome extended to the marvel that (something) is happening, the respect for the event'.[28] I would take that to mean that we must never forget the unpredictable quality of our existence, remaining open to responding to it creatively rather than falling into the trap of thinking that we can ever exert control over it and make it do our bidding. From that point onwards it is a case of figuring away within the hegemonic discourse to disrupt its plans to seduce us, being the rogue element that never lets it rest; that, for Lyotard, is what philosophy really ought to be about (and art too, for that matter), not helping to maintain the status quo just for the sake of it. The morality of the latter course of action has to be open to question, especially if it is for a grand narrative that wants to eradicate its competitors, as so many do, rather than the relativist-based objection to it. Being on the side of the figure within discourse, or of dissension, is not to be amoral: anti-authoritarianism is surely an essential part of any society and Lyotard is one of its most committed advocates, arguing that case persuasively in each of his books, never letting the matter lie. The left in our own day has much to learn from his refusal to give up that fight, especially in terms of its internal relations, where dissent is generally frowned upon and marginalised in the name of party loyalty and a united front (an overpraised phenomenon that so often only leads to dogmatism). Theory ossifies when it is not subjected to dissension, and on a regular basis as well: that is what post-Marxism in general is concerned to make us recognise and act upon. 'How to judge Jean-François Lyotard?': very positively indeed, I would say. The need for figure within discourse becomes ever more apparent in contemporary culture and the case for it has to keep on being made in his spirit: constantly 'prepared to receive what thought is not prepared to think'.

Notes

1. Lyotard, *Lessons on the Analytic of the Sublime*, p. 1; Kant, *Critique of Pure Reason*, *Critique of Practical Reason* and *Critique of Judgment*.
2. Lyotard, *Lessons on the Analytic*, p. 239.
3. Williams, 'Afterword: On Mobled Power', in Grebowicz, *Gender After Lyotard*, pp. 211–20 (p. 212).

4. Lyotard, 'Endurance and the Profession', in *Political Writings*, pp. 70–6 (p. 75).
5. Lyotard, 'Time Today', in *The Inhuman*, pp. 58–77 (p. 73).
6. Lyotard, 'March 23 (Unpublished Introduction to an Unfinished Book on the Movement of March 22)', in *Political Writings*, pp. 60–7 (p. 64).
7. Lyotard, *Discourse, Figure*, p. 18.
8. Lyotard, 'The Sublime and the Avant-Garde', in *The Inhuman*, pp. 89–107 (p. 90).
9. Kant, *Critique of Pure Reason*, p. 394.
10. Lyotard, 'Judiciousness in Dispute, or Kant after Marx', in *The Lyotard Reader*, pp. 324–59 (p. 335).
11. Lyotard, 'A Svelte Appendix to the Postmodern Question', in *Political Writings*, pp. 25–9 (p. 28).
12. Lyotard, *Peregrinations*, p. 5.
13. See Dagnes, *Super Mad at Everything All the Time*.
14. Lyotard and Thébaud, *Just Gaming*, p. 43.
15. Jameson, 'Foreword' to Lyotard, *The Postmodern Condition*, pp. vii–xxi. For Jameson, only a 'genuinely political (and not symbolic or protopolitical) action' can bring about the reform of our current socio-political system, which is the kind of response we would expect a Marxist to make to Lyotard's fairly diffuse political recommendations – here and elsewhere (p. xx).
16. Crome, 'Voicing Nihilism', in Bichis and Shields, *Re-Reading Jean-François Lyotard*, pp. 155–67 (p. 155).
17. Jones and Woodward, 'Setting the Scene', in Jones and Woodward, *Acinemas*, pp. 3–9 (p. 4). Keith Crome notes a sophistic quality to Lyotard's thought in that respect, interpreting sophistry in a more positive sense than its popular usage nowadays would indicate (Crome, *Lyotard and Greek Thought: Sophistry*).
18. Jones, *Lyotard Reframed*, p. 12.
19. See Deleuze and Guattari, *Anti-Oedipus*.
20. Deleuze and Guattari, *A Thousand Plateaus*, p. 380.
21. Ibid., p. 381.
22. Lyotard, *Peregrinations*, p. 3.
23. Lewin, *Complexity*, p. 51.
24. As Graham Jones, for example, notes: 'nowhere in his work does Lyotard provide a *single* definitive account of what the word "event" means. This, I think, is quite deliberate. He seems to suggest that defining it would somehow betray it, would leave out what is important about it' (*Lyotard Reframed*, p. 14). The same would seem to go for all his main concepts, although not all of Lyotard's readers will be as generous towards this lack of clarity as Jones is.
25. Woodward, *Nihilism in Postmodernity*, p. 76. James Williams also emphasises the critical role of nihilism in Lyotard's thought (see Williams,

Lyotard and the Political), as does Keith Crome in 'Voicing Nihilism: Lyotard on Malraux'. The issue has an even wider context for Woodward, for whom 'nihilism arguably remains one of the central problems of contemporary continental philosophy' (Woodward, *Lyotard and the Inhuman Condition*, p. 105). It would seem likely that Marxism's decline could be cited as one of the factors involved.

26. *Waiting for Godot* and *Krapp's Last Tape* would be obvious examples; see Beckett, *The Complete Dramatic Works*.
27. Beckett, *Company*, p. 81.
28. Lyotard, *The Postmodern Explained to Children*, p. 112.

Bibliography

Adair, Gilbert (1992), *The Postmodernist Always Rings Twice*, London: Fourth Estate.

Adorno, Theodor W. [1966] (1973), *Negative Dialectics*, trans. E. B. Ashton, London: Routledge and Kegan Paul.

Adorno, Theodor W. and Max Horkheimer [1944] (1979), *Dialectic of Enlightenment*, trans. John Cumming, London and New York: Verso.

Althusser, Louis (1971), *Lenin and Philosophy and Other Essays*, trans. Ben Brewster, London: New Left Books.

Althusser, Louis and Etienne Balibar [1968] (1970), *Reading Capital*, trans. Ben Brewster, London: New Left Books.

Anderson, Perry (1977), *Considerations on Western Marxism*, London: NLB.

(1961), *The Art of Assemblage: A Symposium*, The Museum of Modern Art, New York, 19 October.

Bamford, Kiff (2012), *Lyotard and the 'Figural' in Performance, Art and Writing*, London and New York: Continuum.

Barthes, Roland (1977), *Image Music Text*, trans. and ed. Stephen Heath, London: Fontana.

Baudrillard, Jean [1973] (1975), *The Mirror of Production*, trans. Mark Poster, St. Louis, MO: Telos Press.

Beasley-Murray, Jon (2011), *Posthegemony: Political Theory and Latin America*, Minneapolis, MN: University of Minnesota Press.

Beauvoir, Simone de [1949] (1972), *The Second Sex*, trans. and ed. H. M. Pashley, Harmondsworth: Penguin.

Beckett, Samuel (1986), *The Complete Dramatic Works*, London: Faber and Faber.

Beckett, Samuel (2009), *Company, Ill Seen Ill Said, Worstword Ho, Stirrings Still*, ed. Dirk Van Hulle, London: Faber and Faber.

Bennington, Geoffrey (1988), *Lyotard: Writing the Event*, Manchester: Manchester University Press.

Bennington, Geoffrey [2005] (2008), *Late Lyotard*, Createspace.

Bichis, Heidi and Rob Shields (eds) (2013), *Re-Reading Jean-François Lyotard: Essays on his Later Works*, Farnham and Burlington, VT: Ashgate.

Bourriaud, Nicolas (ed.) (2009), *Altermodern: Tate Triennial*, London: Tate Publishing.

Brecht, Bertolt [1941] (1981), *The Resistible Rise of Arturo Ui*, trans. Ralph Manheim, eds John Willett and Ralph Manheim, London: Methuen.

Brooks, Michael (2019), 'What's Wrong with the North Pole?', *New Scientist*, 29 June, pp. 34–7.

Carver, Terrell (1998), *The Postmodern Marx*, Manchester: Manchester University Press.

Castoriadis, Cornelius (1987), *The Imaginary Institution of Society*, trans. Kathleen Blamey, Cambridge: Polity Press.

Cixous, Hélène [1975] (1981), 'The Laugh of the Medusa', in Elaine Marks and Isabelle de Courtivron (eds), *New French Feminisms*, Brighton: Harvester, pp. 245–64.

Crome, Keith (2004), *Lyotard and Greek Thought: Sophistry*, Basingstoke and New York: Palgrave Macmillan.

Crome, Keith (2013), 'Voicing Nihilism: Lyotard on Malraux', in Heidi Bichis and Rob Shields (eds), *Re-Reading Jean-François Lyotard: Essays on his Later Works*, Farnham and Burlington, VT: Ashgate, pp. 155–67.

Curtis, Neal (2001), *Against Autonomy: Lyotard, Judgement and Action*, Aldershot and Burlington, VT: Ashgate.

Dagnes, Alison (2019), *Super Mad at Everything All the Time: Political Media and Our National Anger*, London: Palgrave Macmillan.

Davies, Ioan (1998), 'Narrative, Knowledge and Art: On Lyotard's Jewish-ness', in Chris Rojek and Bryan S. Turner (eds), *The Politics of Jean-François Lyotard: Justice and Political Theory*, London and New York: Routledge, pp. 84–101.

Deleuze, Gilles and Félix Guattari [1972] (1983), *Anti-Oedipus: Capitalism and Schizophrenia*, trans. Robert Hurley, Mark Seem and Helen R. Lane, London: Athlone Press.

Deleuze, Gilles and Félix Guattari [1980] (1988), *A Thousand Plateaus: Capitalism and Schizophrenia*, trans. Brian Massumi, London: Athlone Press.

Derrida, Jacques [1967] (1978), *Writing and Difference*, trans. Alan Bass, Chicago: University of Chicago Press.

Derrida, Jacques (1988), *The Ear of the Other: Otobiography, Transference, Translation*, trans. Peggy Kamuf, ed. Christie McDonald, Lincoln, NA and London: University of Nebraska Press.

Derrida, Jacques [1993] (1994), *Specters of Marx: The State of the Debt, The Work of Mourning, and The New International*, trans. Peggy Kamuf, London: Routledge.

Derrida, Jacques [1985] (2018), *Before the Law: The Complete Text of Préjugés*, trans. Sandra van Reenen and Jacques de Ville, Minneapolis, MN and London: University of Minnesota Press.

Descartes, René (1970), *Philosophical Writings*, trans. Elizabeth Anscombe and Peter Thomas Geach, London: Thomas Nelson.

Di Cesare, Donatella [2014] (2018), *Heidegger and the Jews: The Black Notebooks*, trans. Murtha Baca, Cambridge and Medford, MA: Polity Press.

Du Sautoy, Marcus (2019), 'The Q & A', *New Humanist*, 134:3, pp. 6–8.

Farías, Victor [1987] (1989), *Heidegger and Nazism*, eds Joseph Margolis and Paul Rockmore, trans. Paul Burrell and Gabriel R. Ricci, Philadelphia, PA: Temple University Press.

Faye, Emmanuel [2005] (2009), *Heidegger: The Introduction of Nazism into Philosophy, in Light of the Unpublished Seminars*, trans. Michael B. Smith, New Haven, CT: Yale University Press.

Ferguson, Niall (2002), *Empire: How Britain Made the Modern World*, London: Penguin.

Fraser, Nancy and Linda J. Nicholson (1990), 'Social Criticism Without Philosophy', in Linda J. Nicholson (ed.), *Feminism/Postmodernism*, London: Routledge, pp. 19–38.

Frey, Carl Benedikt (2019), *The Technology Trap: Capital, Labor, and Power in the Age of Automation*, Princeton, NJ: Princeton University Press.

Fukuyama, Francis (1992), *The End of History and the Last Man*, London: Penguin.

Gibson, William (1984), *Neuromancer*, London: Victor Gollancz.

Godwin, William [1793] (1985), *Enquiry Concerning Political Justice: And its Influence on Modern Morals and Happiness*, ed. Isaac Kramnick, London: Penguin.

Gordon, Avery [1997] (2008), *Ghostly Matters: Haunting and the Sociological Imagination*, revd edn, Minneapolis, MN and London: University of Minnesota Press.

Gorz, André (1982), *Farewell to the Working Class: An Essay on Post-Industrial Socialism*, trans. Mike Sonenscher, London: Pluto Press.

Gramsci, Antonio (1971), *Selections from the Prison Notebooks*, trans. and ed. Quintin Hoare and Geoffrey Nowell Smith, London: Lawrence and Wishart.

Grebowicz, Margret (ed.) (2007), *Gender After Lyotard*, Albany, NY: State University of New York Press.

Habermas, Jürgen (1989), *The New Conservatism: Cultural Criticism and the Historians' Debate*, ed. and trans. Shierry Weber Nicholsen, Cambridge and Oxford: Polity Press and Blackwell.

Haraway, Donna J. (1991), *Simians, Cyborgs, and Women: The Reinvention of Nature*, New York: Routledge.

Heidegger, Martin (2016), *Ponderings II–VI: Black Notebooks 1931–1938*, trans. Richard Rojcewicz, Bloomington, IN: Indiana University Press.

Heidegger, Martin (2017), *Ponderings VII–XI: Black Notebooks 1938–1939*, trans. Richard Rojcewicz, Bloomington, IN: Indiana University Press.

Heidegger, Martin (2017), *Ponderings XII–XV: Black Notebooks 1939–1941*, trans. Richard Rojcewicz, Bloomington, IN: Indiana University Press.

Hindess, Barry and Paul Q. Hirst (1975), *Pre-Capitalist Modes of Production*, London, Henley and Boston, MA: Routledge and Kegan Paul.

Hindess, Barry and Paul Q. Hirst (1977), *Mode of Production and Social Formation*, London: Macmillan.

Hobbes, Thomas [1651] (1968), *Leviathan, or, The Matter, Forme, and Power of a Free Common-wealth Ecclesiasticall and Civill*, ed. C. B. Macpherson, Harmondsworth: Penguin.

Honneth, Axel [1992] (1995), *The Struggle for Recognition: The Moral Grammar of Social Conflicts*, trans. Joel Anderson, Cambridge: Polity.

Hustvedt, Siri (2019), 'A Woman in the Men's Room: When Will the Art World Recognise the Real Artist Behind Duchamp's Fountain?', *The Guardian*, 29 March, www.theguardian.com/profile/siri-hustvedt-contributor (accessed 15 September 2019).

Irigaray, Luce [1977] (1985), *This Sex Which Is Not One*, trans. Catherine Porter, with Carolyn Burke, Ithaca, NY: Cornell University Press.

Irigaray, Luce [1984] (1993), *An Ethics of Sexual Difference*, trans. Carolyn Burke and Gillian C. Gill, London: Athlone Press.

Irigaray, Luce and Sylvère Lotringer (eds) (2000), *Why Different?: A Culture of Two Subjects. Interviews with Luce Irigaray*, trans. Camille Collins, New York: Semiotext(e).

Jencks, Charles [1975] (1991), *The Language of Post-Modern Architecture*, 6th edn, London: Academy Editions.

Jones, Graham (2014), *Lyotard Reframed*, London and New York: I. B. Tauris.

Jones, Graham and Ashley Woodward (eds) (2017), *Acinemas: Lyotard's Philosophy of Film*, Edinburgh: Edinburgh University Press.

Kant, Immanuel [1787] (1973), *Critique of Pure Reason*, trans. Norman Kemp Smith, London and Basingstoke: Macmillan.

Kant, Immanuel [1788] (2015), *Critique of Practical Reason*, trans. Mary Gregor, Cambridge: Cambridge University Press.

Kant, Immanuel [1790] (2007), *Critique of Judgment*, trans. James Creed Meredith, revd Nicolas Walker, Oxford: Oxford University Press.

Knowles, Adam (2019), *Heidegger's Fascist Affinities: A Politics of Silence*, Stanford, CA: Stanford University Press.

Kosko, Bart (1993), *Fuzzy Thinking: The New Science of Fuzzy Logic*, London: Flamingo.

Lacan, Jacques [1981] (1993), *The Seminar of Jacques Lacan, Book III. The Psychoses 1955–1956*, ed. Jacques-Alain Miller, trans. Russell Grigg, New York and London: W. W. Norton.

Laclau, Ernesto (1990), *New Reflections on the Revolution of Our Time*, London and New York: Verso.

Laclau, Ernesto (2005), *On Populist Reason*, London and New York: Verso.

Laclau, Ernesto [1977] (2011), *Politics and Ideology in Marxist Theory: Capitalism, Fascism, Populism*, London and New York: Verso.

Laclau, Ernesto and Chantal Mouffe (1985), *Hegemony and Socialist Strategy: Towards a Radical Democratic Politics*, London: Verso.

Laclau, Ernesto and Chantal Mouffe (1987), 'Post-Marxism Without Apologies', *New Left Review*, 166, pp. 79–106.

Lewin, Roger (1993), *Complexity: Life on the Edge of Chaos*, London: Phoenix.

Lovelock, James, with Bryan Appleyard (2019), *Novacene: The Coming Age of Hyperintelligence*, London: Penguin.

Lukács, Georg [1922] (1971), *History and Class Consciousness: Studies in Marxist Dialectics*, trans. Rodney Livingstone, London: Merlin Press.

Lyon, James K. (2006), *Paul Celan and Martin Heidegger: An Unresolved Conversation, 1951–1970*, Baltimore, MD: Johns Hopkins University Press.

Lyotard, Dolorès (2012), 'Epilogue', in Jean-François Lyotard, *Writings on Contemporary Art and Artists. Miscellaneous Texts II: Contemporary Artists*, vol. 4, ed. Herman Parret, trans. Vlad Ionescu, Erica Harris and Peter W. Milne, Leuven: Leuven University Press, pp. 687–95.

Lyotard, Jean-François [1979] (1984), *The Postmodern Condition: A Report on Knowledge*, trans. Geoff Bennington and Brian Massumi, Manchester: Manchester University Press.

Lyotard, Jean-François (1984), *Driftworks*, ed. Roger McKeon, trans. Susan Hanson, Richard Lockwood, Joseph Maier, Ann Matejka and Roger McKeon, New York: Semiotext(e).

Lyotard, Jean-François [1983] (1988), *The Differend: Phrases in Dispute*, trans. Georges Van Den Abbeele, Manchester: Manchester University Press.

Lyotard, Jean-François (1988), *Peregrinations: Law, Form, Event*, New York and Oxford: Columbia University Press.

Lyotard, Jean-François (1989), *The Lyotard Reader*, ed. Andrew Benjamin, Oxford and Cambridge, MA: Blackwell.

Lyotard, Jean-François [1988] (1990), *Heidegger and "the jews"*, trans. Andreas Michel and Mark S. Roberts, Minneapolis, MN: University of Minnesota Press.

Lyotard, Jean-François [1977] (1990), *Duchamp's Trans/Formers*, trans. I. McLeod, Venice, CA: Lapis Press.

Lyotard, Jean-François [1988] (1991), *The Inhuman: Reflections on Time*, trans. Geoffrey Bennington and Rachel Bowlby, Stanford, CA: Stanford University Press.

Lyotard, Jean-François [1986] (1992), *The Postmodern Explained to Children: Correspondence 1982–1985*, trans. Don Barry et al., eds Julian Pefanis and Morgan Thomas, London: Turnaround.

Lyotard, Jean-François [1974] (1993), *Libidinal Economy*, trans. Iain Hamilton Grant, London: Athlone Press.

Lyotard, Jean-François (1993), *Political Writings*, trans. Bill Readings and Kevin Paul Geiman, London: UCL Press.

Lyotard, Jean-François [1991] (1994), *Lessons on the Analytic of the Sublime*, trans. Elizabeth Rottenberg, Stanford, CA: Stanford University Press.

Lyotard, Jean-François (1998), *The Assassination of Experience by Painting – Monory*, ed. Sarah Wilson, trans. Rachel Bowlby, London: Black Dog.

Lyotard, Jean-François [1998] (2001), *Soundproof Room: Malraux's Anti-Aesthetics*, trans. Robert Harvey, Stanford, CA: Stanford University Press.

Lyotard, Jean-François (2006), *The Lyotard Reader and Guide*, eds Keith Crome and James Williams, Edinburgh: Edinburgh University Press.

Lyotard, Jean-François (2009), 'Music and Postmodernity', trans. David Bennett, in *New Formations*, 66 (Spring), pp. 37–45.

Lyotard, Jean-François (2009–13), *Writings on Contemporary Art and Artists*, vols 1–6, ed. Herman Parret, Leuven: Leuven University Press.

Lyotard, Jean-François [1971] (2010), *Discourse, Figure*, trans. Antony Hudek and Mary Lydon, Minneapolis, MN and London: University of Minnesota Press.

Lyotard, Jean-François (2012), *Writings on Contemporary Art and Artists. Miscellaneous Texts II: Contemporary Artists*, vol. 4, ed. Herman Parret, trans. Vlad Ionescu, Erica Harris and Peter W. Milne, Leuven: Leuven University Press.

Lyotard, Jean-François [2012] (2013), *Why Philosophize?*, trans. Andrew Brown, Cambridge and Malden, MA: Polity Press.

Lyotard, Jean-François (2017), 'Acinema', trans. Paisley N. Livingstone (modified by Peter W. Milne and Ashley Woodward), in Graham Jones and Ashley Woodward, (eds), *Acinemas: Lyotard's Philosophy of Film*, Edinburgh: Edinburgh University Press, pp. 33–42.

Lyotard, Jean-François (2017), 'Two Metamorphoses of the Seductive', trans. Peter W. Milne and Ashley Woodward, in Graham Jones and Ashley Woodward, (eds), *Acinemas: Lyotard's Philosophy of Film*, Edinburgh: Edinburgh University Press, pp. 59–61.

Lyotard, Jean-François and Jean-Loup Thébaud [1979] (1985), *Just Gaming*, trans. Wlad Godzich, Manchester: Manchester University Press.

Lyotard, Jean-François and Eberhard Gruber [1993] (1999), *The Hyphen: Between Judaism and Christianity*, trans. Pascale-Anne Brault and Michael Naas, Amherst, NY: Humanity Books.

McLennan, Matthew R. (2013), 'Anthro-Paralogy: Antihumanism in Lyotard's Late Works', in Heidi Bichis and Rob Shields (eds), *Re-Reading Jean-François Lyotard: Essays on his Later Works*, Farnham and Burlington, VT: Ashgate, pp. 43–53.

Malpas, Simon (2003), *Jean-François Lyotard*, London and New York: Routledge.

Marx, Karl [1867] (1972), *Capital*, vol. 1, trans. Eden and Cedar Paul, London and New York: Everyman.

Marx, Karl and Friedrich Engels [1848] (1988), *The Communist Manifesto*, ed. Frederic L. Bender, New York and London: W. W. Norton.

Moffitt, Benjamin (2016), *The Global Rise of Populism: Performance, Political Style and Representation*, Stanford, CA: Stanford University Press.

Mouffe, Chantal (2000), *The Democratic Paradox*, London and New York: Verso.

Mouffe, Chantal (2005), *On the Political*, London and New York: Routledge.

Mouffe, Chantal (2018), *For a Left Populism*, London and New York: Verso.

Munck, Ronaldo (2019), 'Democracy without Hegemony: A Reply to Mark Purcell', *Global Discourse*, 9:2, pp. 301–3.

Nicholson, Linda J. (ed.) (1990), *Feminism/Postmodernism*, London: Routledge.

Pierce, David and Peter de Voogd (eds) (1996), *Laurence Sterne in Modernism and Postmodernism*, Amsterdam and Atlanta, GA: Editions Rodopi.

Propp, Vladimir [1928] (1968), *Morphology of the Folktale*, trans. Laurence Scott, rev. and ed. Louis A. Wagner, Austin, TX and London: University of Texas Press.

(2009), *The Protocols of the Elders of Zion*, Eastford, CT: Martino Fine Books.

Pullman, Philip (2019), *The Secret Commonwealth*, London: Penguin.

Purcell, Mark (2019), 'Democracy Beyond Hegemony', *Global Discourse*, 9:2, pp. 285–300.

Readings, Bill (1991), *Introducing Lyotard: Art and Politics*, London and New York, Routledge.

Rockmore, Tom (1992), *On Heidegger's Nazism and Philosophy*, Berkeley, CA and Los Angeles: University of California Press.

Rojek, Chris and Bryan S. Turner (eds) (1998), *The Politics of Jean-François Lyotard: Justice and Political Theory*, London and New York: Routledge.

Rorty, Richard (1982), *Consequences of Pragmatism: (Essays 1972–1980)*, Brighton: Harvester.

Ross, Alex (2007), *The Rest is Noise: Listening to the Twentieth Century*, New York: Farrar, Strauss and Giroux.

Sartre, Jean-Paul [1948] (1967), *What is Literature?*, trans. Bernard Frechtman, London: Methuen.

Sartre, Jean-Paul [1960] (1991), *Critique of Dialectical Reason, Volume I*, trans. Alan Sheridan-Smith, London and New York: Verso.

Scott, Derek B. (2011), 'Postmodernism and Music', in Stuart Sim (ed.), *The Routledge Companion to Postmodernism*, 3rd edn, Abingdon and New York: Routledge, pp. 182–93.

Seidler, Victor J. (1998), 'Identity, Memory and Difference: Lyotard and "the jews"', in Chris Rojek and Bryan S. Turner (eds), *The Politics of Jean-François Lyotard: Justice and Political Theory*, London and New York: Routledge, pp. 102–27.

Sextus Empiricus (1994), *Outlines of Scepticism*, trans. Julia Annas and Jonathan Barnes, Cambridge: Cambridge University Press.

Shelley, Mary [1818] (1980), *Frankenstein, or The Modern Prometheus*, eds James Kinsley and M. K. Joseph, Oxford: Oxford University Press.

Sim, Stuart (2019), *Post-Truth, Scepticism and Power*, London: Palgrave Macmillan.

Standing, Guy (2011), *The Precariat: The New Dangerous Class*, London and New York: Bloomsbury.

Sterne, Laurence [1759–67] (1983), *The Life and Opinions of Tristram Shandy*, ed. Ian Campbell Ross, Oxford: Oxford University Press.

Traverso, Enzo (2016), *Left-Wing Melancholia: Marxism, History, and Memory*, New York and Chichester: Columbia University Press.

Trotsky, Leon [1937] (1965), *The Revolution Betrayed: What is the Soviet Union and Where is it Going?*, trans. Max Eastman, New York: Merit.

Vaughan, Adam (2019), 'Controversial Climate Study Under Investigation', *New Scientist*, 27 July, p. 14.

Vince, Gaia (2019), 'The Chemical-Physical Type of Humanity Has Had Its Time', *New Scientist*, 27 July, pp. 45–7.

Williams, James (1998), *Lyotard: Towards a Postmodern Philosophy*, Cambridge: Polity.

Williams, James (2000), *Lyotard and the Political*, London and New York: Routledge.

Williams, James (2007), 'Afterword: On Mobled Power', in Margaret Grebowicz (ed.), *Gender After Lyotard*, Albany, NY: State University of New York Press, pp. 211–20.

Wilson, Sarah (1998), 'Lyotard/Monory: Postmodern Romantics', in Jean-François Lyotard, *The Assassination of Experience by Painting – Monory*, ed. Sarah Wilson, trans. Rachel Bowlby, London: Black Dog, pp. 19–81.

Winterson, Jeanette (2019), *Frankissstein: A Love Story*, London: Jonathan Cape.

Wolfson, Elliot R. (2018), *The Duplicity of Philosophy's Shadow: Heidegger, Nazism, and the Jewish Other*, New York: Columbia University Press.

Woodward, Ashley (2009), *Nihilism in Postmodernity: Lyotard, Baudrillard, Vattimo*, Aurora, CO: Davies Group.

Woodward, Ashley (2017), *Lyotard and the Inhuman Condition: Reflections on Nihilism, Information and Art*, Edinburgh: Edinburgh University Press.

Zharkova, V., S. Shepherd, S. Zharkov and E. Popova (2019), 'Oscillations of the Baseline of Solar Magnetic Field and Solar Irradiance on a Millennial Timescale', *Scientific Reports*, 24 June.

Žižek, Slavoj (1989), *The Sublime Object of Ideology*, London and New York: Verso.

Index